- INSTALL ELECTRICAL BREAKERS FOR ENTIRE SHOP WITHIN EASY REACH, CIRCUIT-RATED FOR SUFFICIENT AMPERAGE
- STOCK FIRST AID KIT WITH MATERIALS TO TREAT CUTS, GASHES, SPLINTERS, FOREIGN OBJECTS AND CHEMICALS IN EYES, AND BURNS
- HAVE TELEPHONE IN SHOP TO CALL FOR HELP
- INSTALL FIRE EXTINGUISHER RATED FOR A-, B-, AND C-CLASS FIRES
- WEAR EYE PROTECTION AT ALL TIMES
- LOCK CABINETS AND POWER TOOLS TO PROTECT CHILDREN AND INEXPERIENCED VISITORS
- USE DUST COLLECTOR TO KEEP SHOP DUST AT A MINIMUM
- WEAR SHIRT SLEEVES ABOVE ELBOWS
- WEAR CLOSE-FITTING CLOTHES
- WEAR LONG PANTS
- REMOVE WATCHES, RINGS, OR JEWELRY
- KEEP TABLE AND FENCE SURFACES WAXED AND RUST-FREE
- WEAR THICK-SOLED SHOES, PREFERABLY WITH STEEL TOES

CLAMP-ON FINGERBOARD

3"

8½" — 1½"

13½"

HAND-HELD FINGERBOARD

1½"

6" — 2" — 5" — 1½"

3"

14½"

PROTECTION

WEAR FULL FACE SHIELD DURING LATHE TURNING, ROUTING, AND OTHER OPERATIONS THAT MAY THROW CHIPS

WEAR DUST MASK DURING SANDING AND SAWING

WEAR VAPOR MASK DURING FINISHING

WEAR SAFETY GLASSES OR GOGGLES AT ALL TIMES

WEAR RUBBER GLOVES FOR HANDLING DANGEROUS CHEMICALS

WEAR EAR PROTECTORS DURING ROUTING, PLANING, AND LONG, CONTINUOUS POWER TOOL OPERATION

THE WORKSHOP COMPANION™

FINISHING

TECHNIQUES FOR BETTER WOODWORKING

by Nick Engler

Rodale Press
Emmaus, Pennsylvania

Printed in the United States of America on acid-free ∞,
recycled ♲ paper

If you have any questions or comments concerning this
book, please write:
  Rodale Press
  Book Readers' Service
  33 East Minor Street
  Emmaus, PA 18098

About the Author: Nick Engler is an experienced woodworker, writer, and teacher. He worked as a luthier for
many years, making traditional American musical instru-
ments before he founded *Hands On!* magazine. Today, he is
a contributing editor to *Workbench* magazine and has written
over 20 books on the wood arts. He teaches woodworking
at the University of Cincinnati.

Series Editor: Jeff Day
Editors: Roger Yepsen
              Kenneth Burton
Copy Editor: Sarah Dunn
Graphic Designer: Linda Watts
Graphic Artists: Mary Jane Favorite
              Chris Walendzak
Photographer: Karen Callahan
Cover Photographer: Mitch Mandel
Proofreader: Hue Park
Typesetting by Computer Typography, Huber Heights, Ohio
Interior and endpaper illustrations by Mary Jane Favorite
Produced by Bookworks, Inc., West Milton, Ohio

*The author and editors who compiled this
book have tried to make all the contents as
accurate and as correct as possible. Plans,
illustrations, photographs, and text have
all been carefully checked and cross-
checked. However, due to the variability
of local conditions, construction materials,
personal skill, and so on, neither the
author nor Rodale Press assumes any
responsibility for any injuries suffered, or
for damages or other losses incurred that
result from the material presented herein.
All instructions and plans should be carefully studied and clearly understood
before beginning construction.*

Special Thanks to:

Dave Arnold

Crist Benedict

Ideal Custom Millwork
Clayton, Ohio

Mohawk Finishing Products
Amsterdam, New York

Wertz Hardware
West Milton, Ohio

Library of Congress Cataloging-in-Publication Data

Engler, Nick.
  Finishing/by Nick Engler.
        p.   cm. — (The workshop companion)
  Includes index.
  ISBN 0–87596–138–X   hardcover
  1. Wood finishing.   I. Title   II. Series: Engler, Nick.
      Workshop companion.
TT325.E53   1992
684.1'043—dc20   92–2697
                                          CIP

    6 8 10 9 7   hardcover

CONTENTS

TECHNIQUES

TECHNIQUES

1

A DEFINITION OF FINISHING

The first wood finishes were imitations of natural processes. When wounded, trees bleed sap to protect the exposed wood from disease and insects. After a time, this sap hardens to make a glossy, transparent coating. Centuries ago, craftsmen found that they could dissolve this petrified sap or *resin* in alcohol or oil. When they wiped the solution on a wooden surface, the solvents evaporated and the resin hardened into a thin film, forming an attractive coating that protected the surface.

As time passed, craftsmen experimented with hundreds of resins and solvents, both natural and synthetic, creating thousands of finishes. But the purpose of wood finishing has always remained the same. A finish is *a resinous film that protects the wood and enhances its beauty.* When you apply a finish, you spread a resin-bearing solution over the surface of the wood. The resins harden, changing from a liquid to a solid state to form a thin film — a barrier between the wood and its environment.

Once cured, the resinous film protects the wood in several important ways. It helps the wood resist abrasion, scratches, dents, and other wear and tear. The film also provides a barrier to dirt, grime, liquid spills, and other substances that might harm the wood surface. Finally, it slows the absorption and release of moisture by the wood. This does not keep the wood from

slowly expanding and contracting with changes in the relative humidity, but it does prevent the sudden wood movement (and the resulting shock to the project's joinery) that can occur with abrupt changes in the weather.

Furthermore, the film improves both the look and the feel of the wood. Because of the way in which a finish bonds to the surface, it accentuates the wood

grain. Most finishes can also "warm up" the wood color since the resins have a slight amber tint. Depending on your tastes, you can control how the surface reflects the light by polishing the film to a distinctive luster — flat, glossy, or somewhere in between. And once it's polished, the film eliminates minor irregularities in the wood surface, making it smooth to the touch.

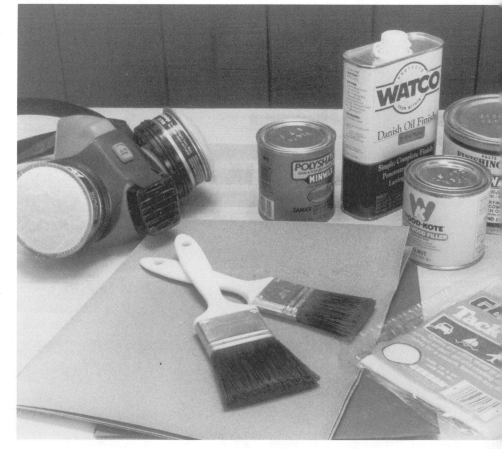

FINISHING AS A DECISION-MAKING PROCESS

The term "finish" encompasses hundreds of finishing materials and processes, each of which has its own distinct effect. Varnish, for example, will protect a wooden surface from spilled alcoholic drinks, while shellac won't. The satin luster of hand-rubbed tung oil is worlds apart from the ultra-high gloss of sprayed lacquer. Furthermore, the degree of protection and enhancement of a particular finish doesn't depend on just its chemistry, but also:

- The species of wood to which the finish is applied
- How the surface of the wood is prepared
- How the finish is applied

There are many variables to consider, many materials and methods you might employ, many effects you can achieve. A successful finish — one that protects the wood and enhances its beauty in the way you had planned — depends on wisely choosing among the alternatives.

Fortunately, although the information you must consider is enormous, the actual finishing is not complex. There are just five steps to applying a finish. (*SEE FIGURE 1-1.*)

1. Select the finish. Ask yourself what kind and what degree of protection you need and what aesthetic effect you want. With a little research and experimentation, you should be able to find the chemicals that will both protect and highlight your project to your satisfaction.

2. Prepare the surface. This is not just a simple matter of sanding and scraping. You must not only smooth the wood surface, but also repair it (where necessary) and clean it thoroughly.

3. Modify the surface. If the color and texture of the wood are acceptable to you, you can skip this step. If not, you may wish to stain, dye, or bleach the wood. Or, fill in the pores and minute imperfections for a supersmooth surface.

4. Apply the finish. There are four basic methods of application — wiping, pouring, brushing, and spraying. You can control many of the protective and aesthetic properties of the finish depending on the technique you use and the number of coats you apply.

5. Finish the finish. Just as you protect and enhance the wood by applying a finish, you can protect and enhance the cured finish with abrasives, glazes, and waxes. Craftsmen disagree whether this final step is necessary. But it doesn't hurt, and these final finishing tasks improve the look and feel of the film.

Take a look at "The Finishing Process: An Overview," the flow chart beginning on page 4. This maps the decision-making maze you must find your way through when finishing a project. It also shows why you can't always follow the simple instructions printed on the sides of finish containers. There are too many variables, and every woodworking project presents a different set. To apply a finish, you must make decisions. To apply a finish properly, you must make *informed* decisions.

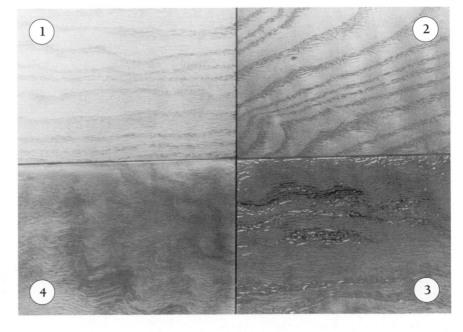

1-1 **These four pieces of red oak** show how a typical finish is built up. *Clockwise from the top left:* (1) After selecting a finish, prepare the surface by smoothing and cleaning it. This board was sanded with 150-grit paper, then wiped with a tack cloth. (2) If necessary, stain, fill, and/or seal the wood — this piece was stained, then the pores were filled with a dark paste wood filler. (3) Apply the finish you have selected. Three coats of polyurethane were applied to this piece. (4) Rub and buff the finish. After the polyurethane hardened completely, this piece was rubbed with rottenstone, then buffed to a high gloss with a paste wax.

THE FINISHING PROCESS: AN OVERVIEW

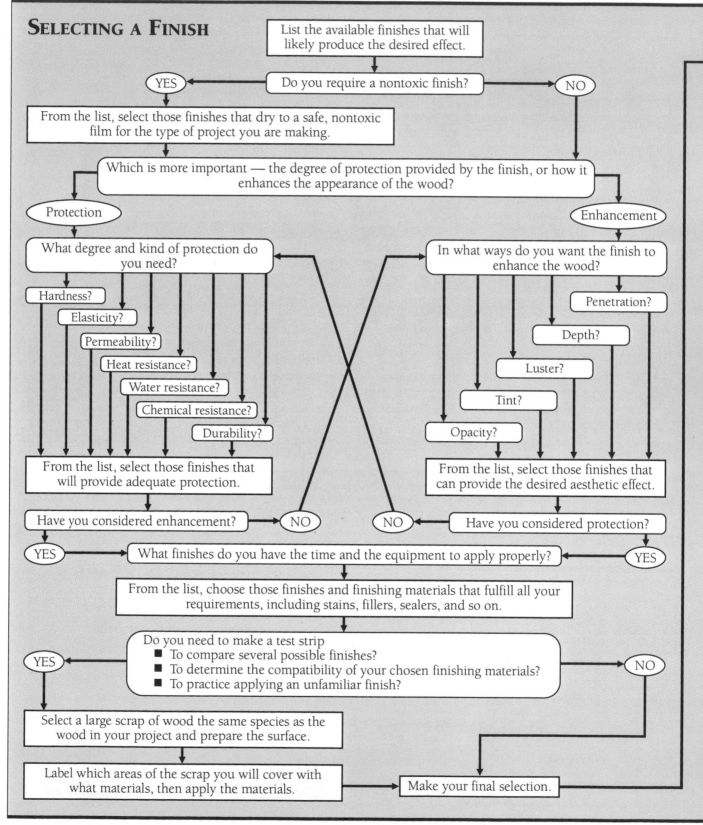

SELECTING A FINISH

List the available finishes that will likely produce the desired effect.

Do you require a nontoxic finish? — YES / NO

YES → From the list, select those finishes that dry to a safe, nontoxic film for the type of project you are making.

Which is more important — the degree of protection provided by the finish, or how it enhances the appearance of the wood?

Protection / Enhancement

What degree and kind of protection do you need?
- Hardness?
- Elasticity?
- Permeability?
- Heat resistance?
- Water resistance?
- Chemical resistance?
- Durability?

In what ways do you want the finish to enhance the wood?
- Penetration?
- Depth?
- Luster?
- Tint?
- Opacity?

From the list, select those finishes that will provide adequate protection.

From the list, select those finishes that can provide the desired aesthetic effect.

Have you considered enhancement? — NO

Have you considered protection? — NO

YES

What finishes do you have the time and the equipment to apply properly?

YES

From the list, choose those finishes and finishing materials that fulfill all your requirements, including stains, fillers, sealers, and so on.

Do you need to make a test strip
- To compare several possible finishes?
- To determine the compatibility of your chosen finishing materials?
- To practice applying an unfamiliar finish?

YES / NO

Select a large scrap of wood the same species as the wood in your project and prepare the surface.

Label which areas of the scrap you will cover with what materials, then apply the materials.

Make your final selection.

NOTE: The information in this chart (and elsewhere in this book) is intended as general or supplemental. Always follow the specific directions provided by manufacturers of finishing materials.

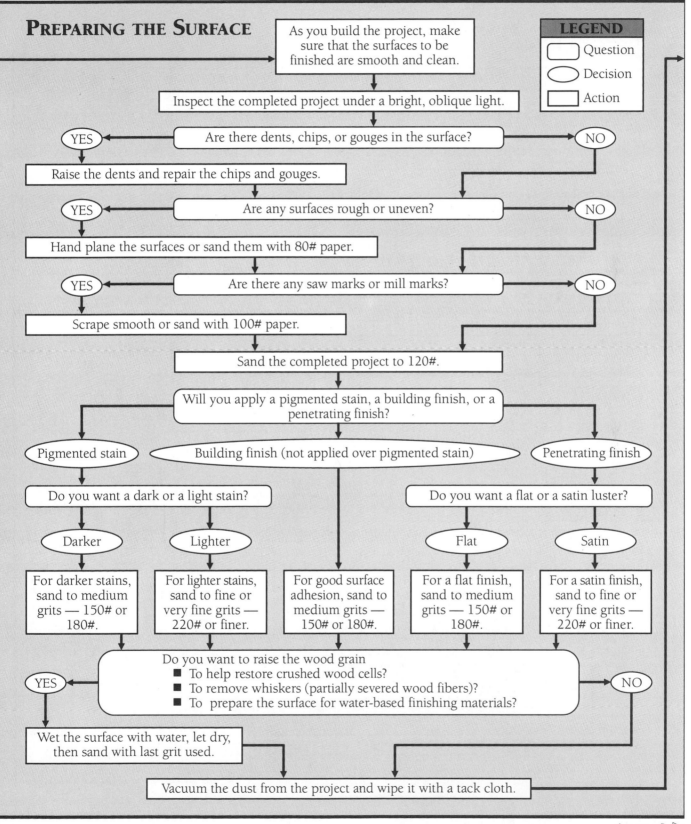

PREPARING THE SURFACE

As you build the project, make sure that the surfaces to be finished are smooth and clean.

Inspect the completed project under a bright, oblique light.

LEGEND
☐ Question
⬭ Decision
☐ Action

Are there dents, chips, or gouges in the surface? — YES / NO

Raise the dents and repair the chips and gouges.

Are any surfaces rough or uneven? — YES / NO

Hand plane the surfaces or sand them with 80# paper.

Are there any saw marks or mill marks? — YES / NO

Scrape smooth or sand with 100# paper.

Sand the completed project to 120#.

Will you apply a pigmented stain, a building finish, or a penetrating finish?

Pigmented stain | Building finish (not applied over pigmented stain) | Penetrating finish

Do you want a dark or a light stain? — Darker / Lighter

Do you want a flat or a satin luster? — Flat / Satin

For darker stains, sand to medium grits — 150# or 180#.

For lighter stains, sand to fine or very fine grits — 220# or finer.

For good surface adhesion, sand to medium grits — 150# or 180#.

For a flat finish, sand to medium grits — 150# or 180#.

For a satin finish, sand to fine or very fine grits — 220# or finer.

Do you want to raise the wood grain
- To help restore crushed wood cells?
- To remove whiskers (partially severed wood fibers)?
- To prepare the surface for water-based finishing materials?

YES / NO

Wet the surface with water, let dry, then sand with last grit used.

Vacuum the dust from the project and wipe it with a tack cloth.

(continued) ▷

THE FINISHING PROCESS: AN OVERVIEW — CONTINUED

MODIFYING THE SURFACE

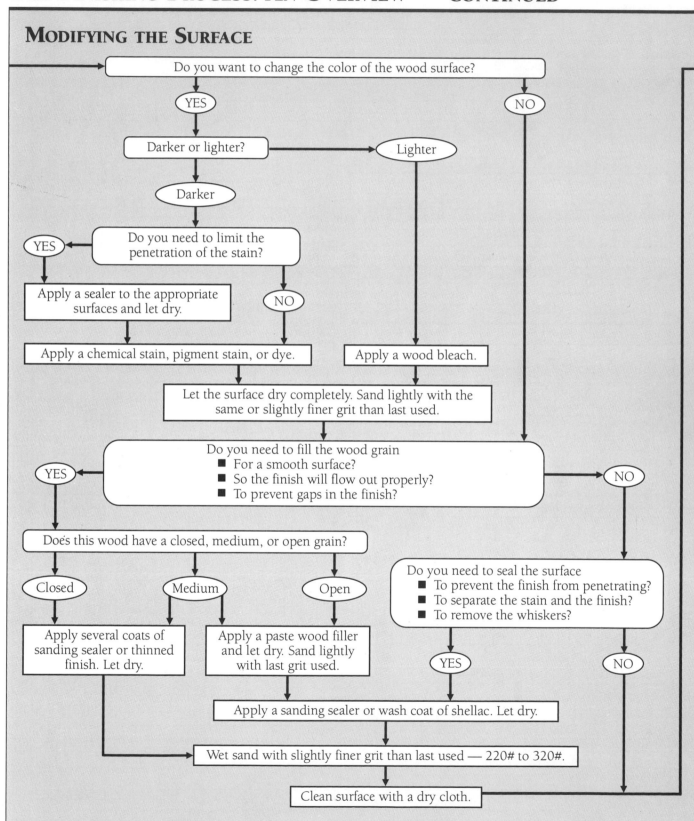

APPLYING THE FINISH

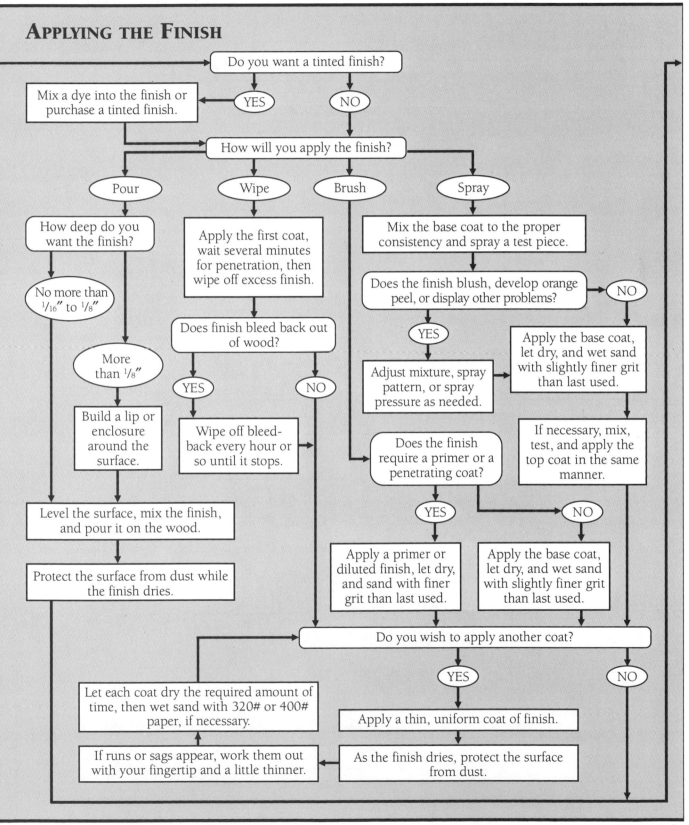

Do you want a tinted finish?

YES — Mix a dye into the finish or purchase a tinted finish.

NO — How will you apply the finish?

Pour — How deep do you want the finish?
- No more than 1/16" to 1/8"
- More than 1/8" — Build a lip or enclosure around the surface.

Level the surface, mix the finish, and pour it on the wood.

Protect the surface from dust while the finish dries.

Wipe — Apply the first coat, wait several minutes for penetration, then wipe off excess finish.

Does finish bleed back out of wood?
- **YES** — Wipe off bleed-back every hour or so until it stops.
- **NO**

Brush — Does the finish require a primer or a penetrating coat?
- **YES** — Apply a primer or diluted finish, let dry, and sand with finer grit than last used.
- **NO** — Apply the base coat, let dry, and wet sand with slightly finer grit than last used.

Spray — Mix the base coat to the proper consistency and spray a test piece.

Does the finish blush, develop orange peel, or display other problems?
- **YES** — Adjust mixture, spray pattern, or spray pressure as needed.
- **NO** — Apply the base coat, let dry, and wet sand with slightly finer grit than last used.

If necessary, mix, test, and apply the top coat in the same manner.

Do you wish to apply another coat?
- **YES** — Apply a thin, uniform coat of finish.

As the finish dries, protect the surface from dust.

If runs or sags appear, work them out with your fingertip and a little thinner.

Let each coat dry the required amount of time, then wet sand with 320# or 400# paper, if necessary.

- **NO**

8

THE FINISHING PROCESS: AN OVERVIEW — CONTINUED

FINISHING THE FINISH

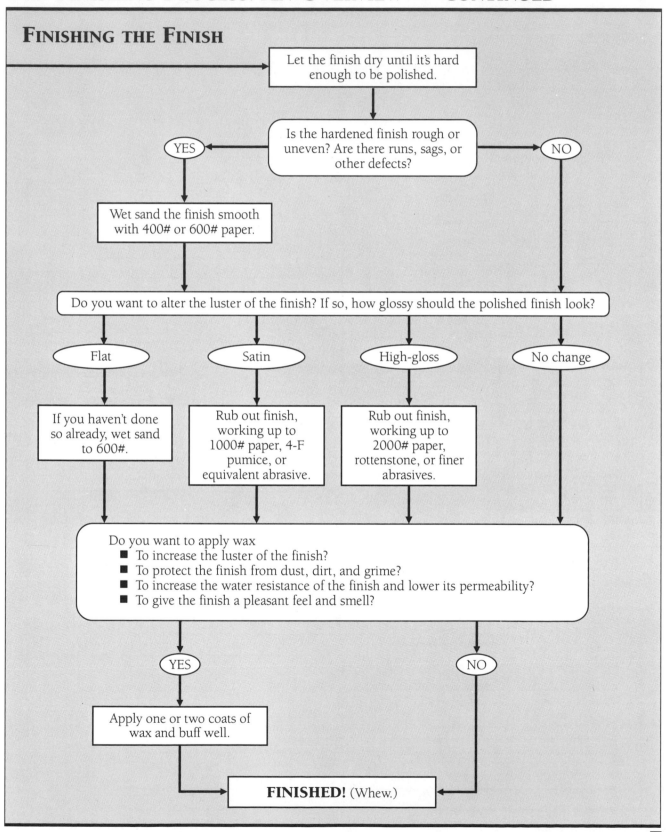

Let the finish dry until it's hard enough to be polished.

Is the hardened finish rough or uneven? Are there runs, sags, or other defects?

YES → Wet sand the finish smooth with 400# or 600# paper.

NO

Do you want to alter the luster of the finish? If so, how glossy should the polished finish look?

Flat — If you haven't done so already, wet sand to 600#.

Satin — Rub out finish, working up to 1000# paper, 4-F pumice, or equivalent abrasive.

High-gloss — Rub out finish, working up to 2000# paper, rottenstone, or finer abrasives.

No change

Do you want to apply wax
- To increase the luster of the finish?
- To protect the finish from dust, dirt, and grime?
- To increase the water resistance of the finish and lower its permeability?
- To give the finish a pleasant feel and smell?

YES → Apply one or two coats of wax and buff well.

NO

FINISHED! (Whew.)

2

UNDERSTANDING FINISHES

To finish a project safely and successfully, it helps to understand how finishes work. Although this is a complex subject, the basics are fairly straightforward. Despite the myriad of finishing choices that overwhelm you in every hardware store, there are more similarities between finishes than there are differences. Take a few minutes to read the labels on a half-dozen cans of finishes and you'll find that different brands —

even different types of finishes — use many of the same chemicals blended in slightly different proportions. You simply need to know what these chemicals are and how they react with wood.

You must also understand how they react with *you,* and how to protect yourself from their harmful effects. Finishes are toxic materials. If used prudently, with the recommended precautions, they are relatively safe. Improperly

used, however, finishes can cause discomfort, disability, even death.

(Sour) Note: Comparing the ingredients and divining the dangers in a few cans of finish presume, of course, that you'll be able to find cans whose labels list the contents. This is becoming increasingly difficult. For more on that subject, see "Labels and Data Sheets: Incomplete Information" on page 14.

How a Finish Works

Walk into any hardware store or thumb through a finishing catalog, and you'll likely find these popular choices:

- *Drying oils* — boiled linseed oil, pure tung oil
- *Rubbing oils* — Danish oil, antique oil, most "tung oil" finishes, salad bowl finish
- *Shellacs* — white shellac, orange shellac
- *Lacquers* — spray lacquer, brush lacquer, lacquer paint
- *Varnishes* — tung oil varnish, spar varnish, varnish stains
- *Polyurethanes* — polyurethane varnish, urethane stain
- *Epoxies* — bar-top finish, epoxy resin
- *Waterborne acrylics* — Water-based varnish, water-based lacquer (sometimes called *water reducible* varnish and lacquer)
- *Oil paints* — spray paint, house paint, artist's oils
- *Latex paints* — interior latex, exterior latex, artist's acrylics

In addition, you'll also find these common finishing materials:

- *Stains* — oil stain, gel stain
- *Wood dyes* — aniline dye, spirit stain
- *Wood fillers* — paste filler, liquid filler
- *Sanding sealers* — lacquer sealer, varnish sealer
- *Waxes* — paste wax, furniture wax

Note: There are many finishing materials, such as wax sticks, stick shellac, wood putty, paint strippers, and so on, that are not included here because they are not necessary parts of a finishing *system* — the various solutions you can apply to a wood surface to create a protective, attractive film.

With a few exceptions, most of these finishes bear little resemblance to the old-time concoctions of natural resins and solvents. Today, they're made from synthetic or highly modified resins with a much higher molecular weight. The solvents, too, have been refined to make more "active" compounds needed to liquify the larger resin molecules. The advantages of these new compounds is that they are easier to apply, quicker to dry, and more durable than their forebears.

BASIC CHEMISTRY

In one important respect, even the newest synthetic finishes are exactly the same as old-time formulas. They still consist primarily of *resins* (sometimes referred to as "solids") and *solvents* (also called "vehicles" or "carriers.") (*See Figure 2-1.*) There are many other chemicals in modern finishes, of course. For example, most include *driers,* heavy metal salts such as cobalt or manganese that speed the drying process. *Flatteners* are extremely fine white or colorless powders, often made from quartz or silica, that give the finish a flat or "satin" look. *Pigments* are colored, opaque powders that tint the finish or stain. And there are others that you might find listed on a label, such as binders, plasticizers, extenders, fillers, hardeners, and so on that affect the characteristics of the finish.

It's not necessary that you know the names or even the purposes of all these additives, unless you wish to mix your own synthetic finishes from scratch. What important is that you understand these materials are grouped into two general categories — *volatile* and

Finishing Chemistry

FINISH	CHEMICAL TYPE	BONDS TO WOOD	BONDS BETWEEN COATS
Drying oils	Reactive	Mechanical	Chemical/mechanical
Rubbing oils	Reactive	Mechanical	Chemical/mechanical
Shellacs	Solvent-releasing	Mechanical	Chemical
Varnishes	Reactive	Mechanical	Chemical/mechanical
Lacquers	Solvent-releasing	Mechanical	Chemical
Polyurethanes	Reactive	Mechanical	Chemical/mechanical
Epoxies	Catalyzing	Mechanical	Mechanical
Waterborne resins	Coalescent	Mechanical	Chemical/mechanical
Oil paints	Reactive	Mechanical	Chemical/mechanical
Latex paints	Coalescent	Mechanical	Chemical/mechanical

nonvolatile. The volatile chemicals are, for the most part, the solvents — the ingredients that keep the finish liquid so you can wipe, brush, pour, or spray it on the wood. After the finish is applied, the volatile chemicals evaporate or dissipate and what's left is everything else — the nonvolatile resins, hardened oils, driers, flatteners, pigments, and so on. These form the resinous film.

2-1 Almost every finish, no matter what its chemical formula, is made up of two important parts. The chemicals that form the solid chemical film are often called the *nonvolatile* chemicals. Those that suspend, dissolve, or somehow keep the first set of chemicals liquid until you apply them to the wood are solvents, carriers, or vehicles, called *volatile* chemicals. Shellac is a classic example of such a formula — the nonvolatile shellac solids are dissolved in a volatile liquid, alcohol. After you apply the finish to the wood, the alcohol evaporates and the solids are left behind to form a hard chemical film. Boiled linseed oil is an exception. This finish consists of just one chemical that serves both functions — the oil is both the carrier and the solid. After you apply the liquid oil to the wood, it reacts with oxygen and solidifies.

FORMING THE FILM

More important than the ingredients, or even the type of finish, is how the liquid finish hardens to form a chemical film. There are four possible reactions (*SEE FIGURES 2-2 THROUGH 2-5*):

■ *Solvent-releasing* — As the solvent evaporates from the finish, it leaves the resin on the wood surface. The resin is not altered chemically; it just changes from a liquid to a solid. It can be dissolved again by applying the same solvent to it. Examples: shellacs and lacquers.

■ *Reactive* — As the thinners evaporate, the resins or oils react with oxygen in the air. As they oxidize, they harden *and* change chemically. This change is permanent; the resins and oils cannot be redissolved by applying the same thinners. Examples: drying oils, rubbing oils, varnishes, polyurethanes, and oil paints.

■ *Catalyzing* — The resins in these finishes also form films by chemical reaction. However, they don't react with the air but with chemical catalysts. The resins must be mixed with hardeners (catalysts) for the film to form. Once the film is cured, it resists almost all solvents. Example: epoxies.

■ *Coalescing* — The finish consists of a resin (usually with a very high molecular weight) suspended in a nonreactive solvent (usually water). In addition, there is a small amount of a second, highly active synthetic solvent (called a "co-solvent" or a *coalescent*)

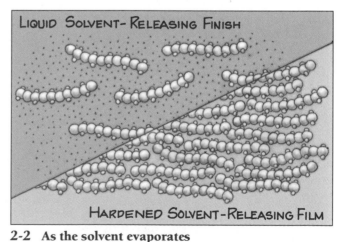

2-2 As the solvent evaporates from a solvent-releasing finish, such as shellac or lacquer, the solids form a solid matrix. However, there is no molecular change and the solids can be easily dissolved again. A fresh coat of finish partially dissolves the old one, and the two coats form a chemical bond.

ील

that keeps the resin liquid. As the water evaporates, the active solvent dissolves the resin and it forms a continuous film. A coalesced film is not as impervious to solvents as reactive finishes, but it cannot be redissolved as easily as solvent-releasing types. Examples: waterborne resins, latex paints.

FOR YOUR INFORMATION

There is a difference between finishes that *harden* and those that *cure*. Finishes in which a chemical reaction takes place, such as reactive and catalyzing finishes, cure. Solvent-releasing and coalescing finishes harden as the solvents dissipate.

In addition to forming films, finishes also form bonds with the wood and — when applied in layers — with themselves. There are two types of bonds:

■ *Chemical bonds* — The molecular structure of the film layer links with that of the wood or the previous layer. These are the strongest (and the most desirable) bonds.

■ *Mechanical bonds* — The finish sticks to the wood or to another finish layer much like adhesive tape, grasping surface irregularities. These bonds are often very weak.

Almost all finishes form mechanical bonds with wood; finishing chemicals do not react with lignin or cellulose, the two major chemical components of wood. For this reason, surface preparation is very important. Ideally, the first coat of finish should penetrate the wood surface slightly, forming what finishing chemists call an "interface," where the two materials interlock.

After the first coat, you must concern yourself with how the finish bonds to itself. Solvent-releasing finishes always form chemical bonds between coats. A newly applied coat partially dissolves the dry coat

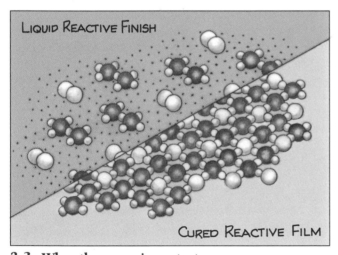

2-3 When they come in contact with oxygen, the resins in reactive finishes such as rubbing oils, varnishes, and polyurethanes form crosslinks, joining up in complex molecular matrices. When the reaction is complete, the solid film is molecularly different from the liquid resin and the reaction cannot be easily reversed. Consequently, the film cannot be dissolved by the same solvent that was used as the vehicle. An additional coat chemically bonds with the preceding one only if the older coat hasn't completely hardened; if it has, the two coats can only form weak mechanical bonds.

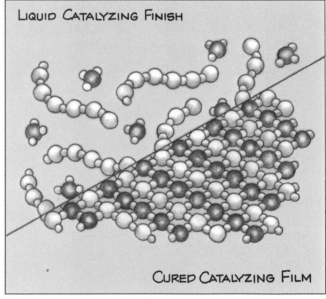

2-4 The resin of a catalyzing finish, such as an epoxy, reacts with a hardener (catalyst) in much the same way reactive resins respond to oxygen. The resin molecules crosslink and form complex matrices that cannot be easily dissolved. Catalyzing finishes are not normally applied in layers. If they are, the same bonding rules apply as for reactive finishes. To achieve strong chemical bonds, you must apply a fresh coat before the old one has completely cured.

underneath it, and the two coats blend into one. Once a catalyzing finish has cured, successive coats will not chemically bond with it — only mechanical bonds will form. Other types — reactive and coalescing finishes — form both chemical and mechanical bonds. If you apply a coat just as the previous coat has set, but before it has a chance to cure (harden completely), then the two layers form strong chemical bonds. After a coat cures, a successive coat can only form mechanical bonds.

When choosing a finish, it's useful to know how various types form films and bonds. Finishes are often built up in several layers, and each layer may have a different chemical formula. Knowing how each layer reacts makes it easier to identify compatible finishing materials. For example, craftsmen often apply a clear finish over a stain. You don't want the chemicals in the finish to dissolve the stain, nor do you want the stain to prevent the finish from hardening.

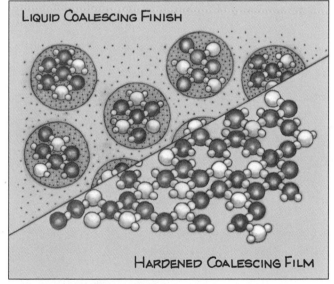

2-5 In its liquid state, a coalescing finish is made up of resins suspended in water and small amounts of an active co-solvent. As the water evaporates, the co-solvent dissolves the resins and forms a continuous film. This film hardens completely as the co-solvent dissipates. The resulting finish is just as hard as many reacted and catalyzed films, but not as resistant to solvents. Successive coats will form both chemical and mechanical coats with preceding ones.

FINISHING SAFETY

In addition to understanding how a finish forms a film on wood, you should also understand what happens when these chemicals come in contact with you. For the most part, finishes are *toxic* to the user. If you limit your exposure to them by following the precautions listed on the sides of containers and in Material Safety Data Sheets, they are relatively safe. But like many of the tools in your shop, if they are used recklessly, they can be dangerous.

CHEMICAL HAZARDS

Most finishes are made with *organic* solvents, so called because they will break down organic hydrocarbons like resins, oils — and you, if you're exposed to them long enough. There are six categories of organic solvents:

■ *Alcohols* — ethanol, methanol, isopropanol
■ *Aliphatic hydrocarbons* — petroleum naphtha, VM&P naphtha, h-Hexane, kerosene
■ *Aromatic hydrocarbons* — toluol, xylene
■ *Chlorinated hydrocarbons* — methylene chloride
■ *Ketones* — acetone, methyl-ethyl ketone, methyl-isobutyl ketone
■ *Others* — turpentine, glycol ether, diglycidyl ether

Most of these toxic materials attack the central nervous system, but some can damage the lungs, liver, kidneys, and blood as well. They will also irritate the skin, eyes, nasal membranes, and throat lining. They can produce both acute and chronic deleterious physical effects.

The acute effects generally last only a short time. An overexposure to high concentrations of finishing chemicals may cause dizziness, shortness of breath, headache, nausea, confusion, incoordination, and irrational behavior. These pass quickly after you remove yourself from the danger. Don't think you can risk an occasional overexposure, however. If the chemicals invade your body in sufficient concentration, the damage can be permanent — or lethal.

The chronic effects can be much more dangerous for two reasons — they sneak up on you, and the damage cannot be reversed. They're usually caused by frequent exposure to low concentrations of chemicals. The effect of each exposure is minor, but it's cumulative. The damage mounts slowly and steadily over the years until the symptoms listed above become a daily ritual. Frequent exposure to high concentrations can cause dementia — loss of memory, impaired judgment, and disorientation.

LABELS AND DATA SHEETS: INCOMPLETE INFORMATION

There was a time when you could get a pretty good idea of what was in a can of finish simply by reading the label. On all but the smallest containers, manufacturers set aside a column or a box with a list of ingredients followed by percentages. Often, these ingredients were divided into "volatile" and "nonvolatile" contents. The volatile contents were mostly solvents, and the nonvolatile contents were resins and other chemicals that helped form the film. The percentages told you how much finish was really in the can. If the nonvolatile contents totaled 33 percent, you knew that two-thirds of the materials would evaporate once you applied the finish.

Unfortunately, this is no longer the case. Increasingly, manufacturers omit the percentages, and the ingredients, if listed at all, are often identified with CAS or TSR numbers. The initials stand for "Chemical Abstract Service" and "Trade Secret Registry." CAS numbers are issued for specific chemical formulas by the Enviromental Protection Agency (EPA), Office of Toxic Substance Assistance. Some states allow manufacturers to substitute TSR for CAS numbers to protect patented formulas.

Often, the list of ingredients is limited to the hazardous chemicals, most of them volatile. And sometimes even those aren't identified by name or number. You can study the labels on many finishing containers only to find that there is a "petroleum distillate" lurking somewhere in the can.

If the labels fail to inform you, you can request a Material Safety Data Sheet from the manufacturer. OSHA requires that these be provided to the user of the finish free of charge. Each sheet is divided into seven sections:

- The *identity* of the finish
- The *hazardous ingredients* in the finish
- The *characteristics* of the finish (boiling point, evaporation rate, appearance, etc.)

1 Oh, for the good old days. The label on this old can of Deft clearly lists the ingredients and the percentages and divides them up between volatile and nonvolatile chemicals. With a little knowledge of finishing chemistry, you can use the label to identify this finish as a brushing lacquer. This, in turn, will help you decide how to prepare the surface and identify compatible finishing materials.

- The *fire and explosion hazards,* if any
- *Reactivity* information (stability, incompatibility, and adverse or dangerous reactions with other chemicals)
- *Health hazards* presented by the chemicals
- *Precautions* for safe handling and use

Unfortunately, these sheets don't always provide you with a complete list of ingredients. The manufacturer is only required to list chemicals that are considered hazardous by OSHA. And the space for percentages is considered optional. In other words, if the manufacturer doesn't want you to know precisely what's in a finish, there's no easy way for you to find out. Most manufacturers will provide you with additional information if you request it, but they are under no obligation to give you a complete list of ingredients.

To be fair, this situation is not entirely the manufacturers' fault. In recent years, state and federal regulations have required increasingly detailed warnings on finish containers. Because these containers are only so big, the available area for directions, ingredients, and other information has shrunk. Furthermore, manufacturers must protect the finishing recipes they've worked hard to develop.

But incomplete labels do not serve the woodworker well, and leave room for fraud. While most manufacturers are trustworthy, there are now finishes on the market whose labels hint at being polyurethanes even though they contain no plastic resins. Similarly, some "tung oil" finishes contain little (if any) real tung oil.

In short, the issue has grown increasingly complex, and the present situation is not satisfactory to either the manufacturer or the craftsman.

2 **The label on this can of "gel** finish" clearly lists the ingredients, but gives no percentages — only CAS and TSR numbers, which are of little value to most craftsmen. How much resin will be left behind when the solvents evaporate? There's no way for you to tell.

3 **The label on the front of this** can identifies the contents as "wipe-on tung oil clear wood finish." Just what is that, anyway? How much tung oil does it contain? What stains and other finishing materials will be compatible? There's no way for you to tell from the label alone.

(continued) ▷

LABELS AND DATA SHEETS: INCOMPLETE INFORMATION — CONTINUED

MSDS Used To Comply With OSHA HAZARD COMMUNICATION STANDARD 29CFR 1910.1200

SECTION V Reactivity Data

| Stability | Stable | X | Conditions to Avoid: | N/A |
| | Unstable | | | |

Incompatibility (Materials to Avoid): Oxidizing materials can cause a vigorous reaction.

Hazardous Decomposition or By-products: Combustion will produce fumes, smoke, carbon dioxide and probably carbon monoxide.

| Hazardous | May Occur | | Conditions to Avoid: | N/A |
| Polymerization | Will Not Occur | X | | |

SECTION VI Health Hazard Data

| Route(s) of Entry: | Eyes? X | Inhalation? X | Skin? X | Ingestion? X |

Health Hazards: Harmful if inhaled, may affect the brain or nervous system, causing dizziness, headache or nausea. Causes nose, throat, eye and skin irritation. Reports have associated repeated and prolonged occupational over-exposure to solvents with permanent brain and nervous system damage. Intentional misuse by deliberately concentrating and inhaling the contents may be harmful or fatal.

| Carcinogenicity: | No | NTP? | N/L | IARC Monographs? N/L | OSHA Regulated? N/L |

Signs and Symptoms of Exposure: Breathing difficulty, dizziness, light-headedness, dryness of respiratory tract.

Medical Conditions Aggervated by Exposure: Any medical condition, allergy, sensitization which may become worse upon exposure to the product.

Emergency and First Aid Procedures:

In Eyes: Flush immediately with large amounts of water for 15 min. T

If Breathed: Remove to fresh air, restore breathing. Consult a physi

If In Skin: Wash areas with soap and water. Remove contaminated

If Swallowed: Dilute by drinking 2 glasses of water. Do not induce v

SECTION VII Precautions for Safe Ha

Steps to be taken In Case Material Is Released or Spilled: Isolate, abso doors). Removal of all ignition sources, flames, hot surfaces. Avoid device.

Waste Disposal Method: In accordance with federal, state and local re to hazard caution information in other sections of the form.

Handling and Storing Precautions: Avoid high temperatures. Keep clo or use near heat, sparks or flame. Prevent prolonged or repeated br

Other Precautions: Do not take internally. Avoid prolonged contact wi breathing of vapors or dust. Keep out of reach of children! Follow la

SECTION VIII Control Measures

Respiratory Protection (Specify Type)	Respirator, cartridge type NI
Ventilation:	Local Exhaust:	Not Adequate
	Mechanical	Sufficient to prevent exceeding lis
Protective Gloves:	Neoprene (Hazard B or greater)	Eye Pr
Other Protective Clothing or Equipment:	N/A
Work/Hygenic Practices:	Follow good housekeeping and personal hygiene

---

M610F

MATERIAL SAFETY DATA SHEET

HAZARD RATING	Flammability
4-SEVERE HAZARD	
3-SERIOUS HAZARD	Reactivity
2-MODERATE HAZARD	1 3 0
1-SLIGHT HAZARD Health	B
0-MINIMAL HAZARD	Personal
(See Section IV)	Protection

| PRODUCT NAME: | Sanding Sealer | PRODUCT NUMBER: |

SECTION I Identity

General ID:	Sealer	Emergency Phone #
D.O.T. Hazard Class:	Flammable Liquid	Information Phone #
D.O.T. Flammability Class:	3	Date Prepared:
Shipping ID:	Guide:	Signature of Preparer

SECTION II Hazardous Ingredients/ Identity Information

HAZARDOUS COMPONENTS	CAS No.	OSHA PEL	ACGIH TLV TWA	Other Limits Recommended	★	% (Optional)
Isopropyl Alcohol	67-63-0	400 PPM	400 PPM	980 mg/M³	*	6.0%
Toluene	108-88-3	100 PPM	100 PPM	375 mg/M³	*	37.0%
Ethanol	64-17-5	1000 PPM	1000 PPM	1900 mgh/M³		> 1.0%
Methyl Ethyl Ketone	78-93-3	200 PPM	200 PPM	590 mg/M³	*	14.0%
Methyl Isobutyl Ketone	108-10-1	50 PPM	50 PPM	205 mg/M³	*	12.0%
Acetone	67-64-1	750 PPM	750 PPM	1780 mg/M³	*	3.0%
Ethyl Acetate	141-78-6	400 PPM	400 PPM	1400 mg/M³		> 1.0%
Isobutyl Isobutyrate	97-85-8	N\L	N\L	N\L		> 1.0%
Isopropyl Acetate	108-21-4	250 PPM	250 PPM	950 mg/M³		> 1.0%
Butyl Acetate	123-86-4	150 PPM	150 PPM	710 mg/M³		> 1.0%

SECTION III Physical/Chemical Characteristics

Boiling Point	160°F	Specific Gravity (H₂O-1)	.92
Vapor Pressure (mm Hg)	76 mm	Melting Point	N/A
Vapor Density (AIR-1)	> 1.0	Evaporation Rate (Butyl Acetate-1)	.8
Solubility in Water	Partial	Appearance and Odor	Semi-opaque, straw colored liquid, aromatic odor

SECTION IV Fire and Explosion Hazard Data

| Flash Point (T.C.C.) | 44°F | Flammable Limits | | LEL 1.9% | UEL | 9.0% |

Extinguishing Media Water spray, "alcohol" foam, dry chemical, foam, CO² or any Class B extinguishing agent.

Special Fire Fighting Procedures Wear self-contained breathing apparatus when fire fighting in confined space. If water is used, fog nozzles are preferred.

Unusual Fire and Explosion Hazards Vapors are heavier than air, may travel considerable distance to a source of ignition and flashback. Use water fog to cool containers to prevent rupturing.

MSDS Form used to comply with OSHA HAZARD COMMUNICATION STANDARD 29 CFR 1910.1200
* Denotes SARA 313 List Component.

4 **Manufacturers must provide** a Material Safety Data Sheet on any finish that contains hazardous materials. These sheets provide much useful information on safety and compatibility. However, they still don't necessarily tell you *what's in the can.*

These chemicals enter your body in several ways. Food and beverages can be easily contaminated, presenting a hazard if you eat or drink in the shop. These chemicals can also enter your body through cuts and abrasions; a few can be absorbed directly through the skin. However, the most common way in which they invade your body is through the lungs — you breathe them in. The amount of tissue exposed with each breath is enormous; the lungs have over two acres of surface area!

All organic solvents are volatile to one degree or another. They will evaporate and fill the air. This volatility is determined by the vapor pressure (VP) generated as the solvents evaporate. It's measured by how many millimeters the pressure will cause a column of mercury to rise (mm HG). The higher the vapor pressure, the faster the fumes fill the air.

Solvents also have different degrees of toxicity. Some have to be present in larger quantities than others to pose a health risk. Toxicity is determined by the threshold limit value (TLV) — how much of the solvent must be present in a given volume of air for it to have a toxic effect. This is generally measured in parts per million (PPM). The lower the threshold PPM, the more toxic the solvent.

The health risk posed by a specific solvent is determined by both its toxicity and its volatility. A highly toxic solvent may be relatively safe if its volatility is low enough. If it doesn't evaporate into the air, and you take care not to ingest it or let it touch your skin, then you won't be exposed to high enough quantities to suffer a harmful effect. By the same token, a solvent with low toxicity and high volatility can be extremely dangerous. If it quickly fills the air with fumes, you may be overexposed in a very short time. The most dangerous solvents are those that are highly toxic and highly volatile; the safest have low toxicity and low volatility.

In addition to posing health risks, most finishing chemicals are also *flammable*. Their flammability varies, but all of the organic solvents listed here can be ignited by a careless spark. Furthermore, linseed oil and some oil-derived products may spontaneously combust *at room temperature* if the vapors are sufficiently concentrated in the air.

HOW TO PROTECT YOURSELF

Use the finish that provides the protection and enhancement that you want and has the less dangerous solvents. For example, if you determine that either a shellac finish or a lacquer finish will work well for you, choose shellac. The alcohol in shellac is decided-

ly less dangerous than the aromatic hydrocarbons and ketones present in lacquer. To help you decide, the "Hazardous Finishing Chemicals" chart on page 20 ranks common solvents from the most dangerous to the least dangerous.

A SAFETY REMINDER

Pregnant and breast-feeding women should avoid *all* organic solvents. Exposure may be especially dangerous to the fetus during the first three months of a pregnancy.

However, it's not enough to choose a relatively safe finish. The chemicals in even the least dangerous products still pose some health risk and fire hazard. You must take additional steps to protect yourself.

Perhaps the most important is to *ventilate the finishing area*. Open the windows; use a fan to keep the air moving. This will help to clear the area of fumes before they have a chance to reach a toxic or combustible concentration. Ventilation is especially important in small shops, or if you have set aside a small room for finishing. Fumes become quickly concentrated in small spaces. Also, some fumes are heavier than air and fall to the floor. For this reason, set the fan on the floor or direct air downward.

If you can, *work outdoors* when using highly volatile chemicals such as acetone or methylene chloride, or when working with large quantities of organic solvents. An open window and a fan may not ventilate the area quickly enough. The fumes might fill an area faster than the air can be evacuated.

If you spray finishes with volatile organic solvents, such as varnish or lacquer, you must *use an explosion-proof spray booth*. As you spray, microscopic droplets of finish — the *overspray* — fill the air. Not only is a spray booth ventilated to carry the fumes outside, the fan motors, lights, and switches are also shielded to prevent an electric spark from igniting the overspray.

A SAFETY REMINDER

It's impossible to overestimate the dangers of spraying a flammable finish, or the importance of explosion-proof wiring in a spray booth. One-half cup of lacquer, when vaporized and mixed with the proper amount of air, has the explosive force of *one stick of dynamite.*

In addition to providing ventilation, you should also *wear a respirator*, particularly if you are spraying finishes or will be exposed to the fumes for over an hour. Don't try to get by with a dust mask; it will not screen out the harmful chemicals from the air you breathe. *(SEE FIGURE 2-6.)* Use a close-fitting mask with filter cartridges rated for organic vapors and a pre-filter for dusts and mists. Make sure both the mask and cartridges are jointly approved by the National Institute for Occupational Safety and Health (NIOSH) and the Mine Safety and Health Administration (MSHA). Replace the cartridges after their useful working time has expired. Keep them in an airtight

container such as a plastic bag when not in use. This will help extend their useful life.

Sometimes a respirator isn't enough. As the chart of "Hazardous Finishing Chemicals" on page 20 shows, many organic solvents can irritate the skin and eyes. When there is danger of splashing or when exposed to these chemicals for long stretches, *wear a full face shield and rubber gloves* in addition to a respirator. You may also wish to apply a *barrier cream* to your skin, especially when working with finishes that contain glycol ether and diglycidyl ether. This skin lotion, which is available from most industrial suppliers, protects flesh from casual contact with harmful chemicals.

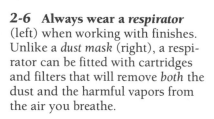

TRY THIS TRICK

Because respirator cartridges wear out after a specific amount of time in use, they must be replaced periodically. However, when you use a respirator only once in a while, it's easy to lose track of the time you've logged. To aid your memory, put a piece of masking tape on the outside of the mask and tick off the hours on the tape. When you replace the cartridges, replace the tape too.

2-6 Always wear a *respirator* (left) when working with finishes. Unlike a *dust mask* (right), a respirator can be fitted with cartridges and filters that will remove *both* the dust and the harmful vapors from the air you breathe.

Be careful how you store these chemicals. *Keep both unused and used finishes and related products in sealed metal containers.* The containers, of course, should have labels. The same precaution applies to rags and paper towels saturated with volatile chemicals, although you don't need to label them. Vapor easily accumulates in the folds of the material and may be ignited by a stray spark. Or, if rags are saturated with linseed oil, they may ignite spontaneously. A sealed metal container insulates rags from sparks, and any spontaneous fire will quickly use up all the oxygen and die before it can spread.

In addition to being careful how you store these chemicals, also *be careful how you dispose of them.*

Depending on the toxicity of the solvent, a single cup — no more than you'd use to clean a brush — can pollute over a thousand gallons of water! Save slightly used solvents, let the solids settle out of them, and use them again.

When they really are used up, take them to an appropriate agency for safe disposal. Call the United States Environmental Protection Agency, Resource Conservation and Recovery Hotline at 1-800-424-9346 to find out who handles chemical disposal in your area. And once again, always choose the least dangerous chemical for the job. The finish that poses the least risk to you will also pose the least risk to the environment.

CLEANER AIR, SAFER FINISHES

The latest addition to the finishing products in your hardware store are *waterborne resins,* commonly called water-based finishes. These are the result of growing environmental concern. Since the early 1960s, most states have passed clean-air legislation that limits the volatile organic compounds (VOC) in finishing products, and the rest are sure to follow.

There are two ways in which finish manufacturers can comply with these laws. They can reduce the percentages of toxic solvents in conventional finishes or develop new low-VOC finishes. So far, the most promising route seems to be new finishes such as the waterborne resins. The carrier in these finishes is *mostly* water, although many still contain as much as 5 percent organic solvents.

In addition to being safer and less toxic, waterborne resins have other advantages. They're almost completely clear, they dry quickly, and they become very hard. They have no unpleasant odor, and you can clean your brushes with soap and water. But they have disadvantages, too. Because they are mostly water, they raise the wood grain. The wood surface must be completely free of oil, grease, and wax for the resins to bond properly. And they are expensive — almost twice the price of conventional finishes.

Whatever the relative advantages and disadvantages, we are likely to see more of these waterborne resins and other low-VOC finishes as the VOC regulations continue to tighten. Will we see less of the familiar varnishes, lacquers, polyurethanes, and other toxic, solvent-based finishes? Probably, for several different reasons:

■ The EPA and other regulatory agencies have outlawed certain *chemical processes* that were found to be polluting. For example, the high-temperature reactions needed to create certain hard resins were forbidden, and finish manufacturers filled the gaps with newer, more benign processes. This has changed — and will continue to change — finishing chemistry.

■ Medical research continues to identify widely-used chemicals as *carcinogens* — cancer-causing agents. Several years ago, the use of the solvent benzene was prohibited for this reason. Soon, the availability of toluol, turpentine, and aniline dyes may be restricted because exposure to them may cause cancer.

■ Presently, most VOC regulations are aimed at industrial users — furniture manufacturers and other companies that use one gallon of finish or more per day. These laws don't directly affect small shops and individual craftsmen. But as industrial users buy less solvent-based finishes from manufacturers, the demand will drop. And sooner or later, so will the supply. It's likely that varnishes, lacquers, and polyurethanes will become increasingly scarce on hardware store shelves.

HAZARDOUS FINISHING CHEMICALS (Ranked in Decreasing Order of Danger to Health)

NAME	CHEMICAL TYPE	USES	TOXICITY (TLV in PPM)*
EXTREMELY DANGEROUS			
1. Methylene Chloride	Chlorinated hydrocarbon	Paint strippers, furniture refinishers, paints	50
2. Glycol Ether‡	Other	Lacquers, dyes, latex paints, spray paints, epoxies	5
3. Diglycidyl Ether‡	Other	Epoxies	0.1
4. n-Hexane	Aliphatic hydrocarbon	Varnishes, rubbing oils	50
MODERATELY DANGEROUS			
5. Methanol	Alcohol	Paints, varnishes, lacquers, dyes, furniture refinishers, paint strippers	200
6. Acetone	Ketone	Paint strippers, wood fillers, lacquers, epoxies	750
7. Methyl-Ethyl Ketone	Ketone	Lacquers, wood fillers, spray paints	200
8. Petroleum Naphtha	Aliphatic hydrocarbon	Wood fillers, waxes, lacquers, general solvents	100
9. Toluol	Aromatic hydrocarbon	Polyurethanes, spray paints, rubbing oils, furniture refinishers, paint strippers, general solvents	100
10. Isopropanol	Alcohol	Wood fillers, lacquers	400
11. Methyl Isobutyl Ketone	Ketone	Wood fillers, spray paints	50
MILDLY DANGEROUS			
12. Xylene	Aromatic hydrocarbon	Lacquers, paint strippers, general solvents	100
13. VM&P Naphtha§	Aliphatic hydrocarbon	Lacquers, varnishes, general solvents	300
14. Turpentine	Other	Waxes, drying oils, rubbing oils, varnishes, general solvents	100
15. Mineral Spirits	Aliphatic hydrocarbon	Wood fillers, rubbing oils, varnishes, polyurethanes, stains, general solvents	200
16. Kerosene	Aliphatic hydrocarbon	General solvents	None
17. Ethanol	Alcohol	Shellacs, stains	1000

*Stands for "Threshold Limit Value in Parts Per Million."
†Stands for "Vapor Pressure in millimeters of Mercury."

VOLATILITY (VP in mm HG)†	DANGERS	SYMPTOMS OF OVEREXPOSURE
350	Affects skin, upper respiratory tract, blood, central nervous system, liver	Irritation, narcosis, numbness, heart palpitations, headache, shortness of breath, angina, heart attack
6	Affects skin, eyes, upper respiratory tract, central nervous system, kidneys, liver, reproductive system, blood	Headache, irritation, narcosis, kidney damage, pulmonary edema, fatigue, anemia
0.09	Affects skin, eyes, central nervous system, reproductive system	Irritation, allergies
124	Affects skin, upper respiratory tract, entire nervous system	Irritation, numbness, weakness, headache, nausea, loss of balance, weight loss, fatigue
97	Affects eyes, skin, central nervous system	Vision problems, optic nerve damage, blindness, narcosis
266	Affects skin, upper respiratory tract, central nervous system, eyes	Irritation, narcosis, dermatitis
70	Affects skin, upper respiratory tract, central nervous system	Irritation, narcosis, dermatitis
40	Affects eyes, skin, upper respiratory tract, lungs, central nervous system	Irritation, narcosis, dermatitis
22	Affects central nervous system, liver, upper respiratory tract, kidneys, skin, eyes	Irritation, dermatitis, narcosis, weakness, liver and kidney damage
33	Affects skin, upper respiratory tract, central nervous system	Irritation, headache, drowsiness
15	Affects skin, upper respiratory tract, central nervous system	Irritation, narcosis, dermatitis
9	Affects skin, upper respiratory tract, central nervous system, liver, gastrointestinal system, blood	Irritation, narcosis, dermatitis, stomach pain, incoordination, staggering
2–20	Affects skin, central nervous system, lungs	Irritation, dermatitis, narcosis
5	Affects skin, eyes, upper respiratory tract, lungs, central nervous system, kidneys, bladder	Irritation, dermatitis, pulmonary edema, narcosis, convulsions, kidney and bladder damage, fever
0.8	Affects skin, central nervous system, lungs, eyes	Irritation, dermatitis, narcosis
Varies	Affects skin, upper respiratory tract, lungs, central nervous system	Irritation, narcosis, lung hemorrhage, chemical pneumonia
43	Affects eyes, nose, skin, central nervous system	Irritation, headache, drowsiness, fatigue

†Although the volatility of these substances is low, they can be absorbed quickly through the skin. Even rubber gloves provide little protection.
§Stands for "Varnish Makers and Painters." This is petroleum naphtha with the more harmful hydrocarbons removed.

3

SELECTING A FINISH

Like most woodworkers, you probably use a few favorite finishes that produce consistently good results for you. When it comes time to choose a finish for a project, you naturally gravitate toward what has worked well for you in the past. After all, why mess with success?

Or you learn about a finish that you'd like to try: It's easy to apply, stands up to hard use, imitates an antique patina, or offers other qualities that capture your interest. Whatever the reason, you resolve to use it whenever the next opportunity arises. In some cases, you may build a project just so you can try the finish.

But what about those occasions when you know the *results* you want from a finish — water resistance, durability, luster, tint, and so on — but don't know how to achieve them? When this is the case, you must do a little research. First, define the results you want — how the finish should enhance the wood and what sort of protection it should afford. Review the available finishing materials and choose those that will create the desired effects. Finally, test these materials to determine if they will indeed produce the results you expect.

QUESTIONS AND ANSWERS

Finishing research needn't be a time-consuming, complex venture. In most cases, it's a simple matter of regrouping the finishes in your mind to identify those that will produce the desired effect. For example:

■ If the depth of a finish (or lack of it) is important, group the choices into *penetrating* finishes that soak into the wood and *building* finishes that form a film on top of it.

■ If the project will be exposed to water, decide whether this exposure will be constant or occasional. Group the finishes into *water sensitive, water resistant,* and *waterproof.*

■ To preserve or enhance the natural color of the wood, determine which finishes are clear and which have a natural amber or artificial tint.

To group the finishes for specific results, study the labels on the containers, read additional information provided by the manufacturer, or consult "Properties of Common Finishes" on page 28.

To narrow your choices between a few appropriate finishes, ask yourself these questions:

■ Do you need a nontoxic finish?

■ Which is more important, enhancement or protection?

■ What enhancing properties do you need?

■ What protecting properties do you need?

■ How much time and what equipment are needed to apply a finish?

Answer the questions in turn, eliminating those finishes that do not provide the specific qualities you're looking for. In the end, you'll be left with just a few likely choices.

DO YOU NEED A NONTOXIC FINISH?

It's best to ask yourself this question first, for two reasons. Because there are so few nontoxic finishes, you can quickly narrow your choices if that's what you need. And more importantly, when making eating utensils, toys, or children's furniture, your overriding concern should be the safety of the folks who will use these objects.

In addition to being toxic when you apply them, finishes may remain toxic after they've dried. Although the organic solvents evaporate, the resins and other nonvolatile substances remain. Most of these are not harmful by themselves, but some are. Heavy metal salts, for example — driers — can be poisonous.

Usually, this residual toxicity poses no threat. But if these chemicals are ingested, they can be dangerous.

When chewed or abraded by knives and forks, the finish can flake off and be swallowed. Or, the mild acids in saliva and food juices may leach the finish out of the wood. To be safe, use finishes that retain little or no toxicity after curing.

■ The traditional nontoxic finish is *mineral oil.* Unfortunately, mineral oil does not dry and you must periodically reapply it to the wood for continued protection.

■ You can also use *walnut oil,* which does dry but does not form a hard film. Walnut oil is available at most health food stores, and several commercial finishes are made with nut oils.

■ *Shellac,* in solid form, is nontoxic. But most commercially mixed shellacs contain driers or methanol. In order to make a nontoxic shellac, cut pure shellac flakes with hydrous ethyl alcohol.

■ Manufacturers of *Danish oil* claim that it's nontoxic when fully cured. However, it takes 30 days to cure completely. This is not the finish to throw on the kids' toys the night before Christmas.

■ *Salad bowl finishes* are manufactured from FDA-approved chemicals and foodstuffs. They're durable, but like nut oils, they do not form hard films.

■ Several brands of *waterborne resins* are marketed as nontoxic. Because they flake off, they're not recommended for eating utensils. But they are safe for children's furniture and playthings.

■ Finally, *milk paint* is relatively benign. It's not recommended for eating utensils or objects that will be used by infants, but it's safe for playthings and furniture that will be used by older children, age three and up. (See "Reproducing Antique Finishes" on page 24.)

WHERE TO FIND IT

Although some of these finishes may be available from local stores, most — including shellac flakes and ethyl alcohol — must be ordered through the mail. Here are several suppliers:

Woodcraft Supply
41 Atlantic Avenue
P.O. Box 4000
Woburn, MA 01888

Constantine's
2050 Eastchester Road
Bronx, NY 10461

Garrett Wade
161 Avenue of the Americas
New York, NY 10013

REPRODUCING ANTIQUE FINISHES

If you like to build antique reproductions — early classic and country furniture — you may wish to apply a historically correct finish. When a transparent finish was called for, old-time craftsmen often rubbed boiled linseed oil into the wood surface, following this traditional schedule: "Twice a day for a week, twice a week for a month, then twice a year forever." Or they mixed equal parts of beeswax and turpentine to make a paste and rubbed several coats into the wood, buffing each coat. Like linseed oil, this wax finish had to be reapplied several times yearly.

For special pieces and well-to-do clients, the woodworkers mixed varnishes from natural resins such as copal, gum mastic, rosin, sandarac, and dragon's blood. All of these are soluble in either linseed oil, alcohol, or both. Each craftsman had his own special blend whose ingredients he jealously guarded, and few of these recipes have survived.

To mix an old-time varnish of your own, you must duplicate the same trial-and-error process that most eighteenth- and nineteenth-century cabinetmakers went through, testing various mixtures before settling on one that seems superior.

In addition to being oiled and varnished, many old-time furniture pieces were painted. The most popular furniture paint was *milk paint,* which used the gluelike substance in milk — called *casein* — as a binder. When mixed with lime and linseed oil and tinted with a powdered pigment, milk forms a remarkably versatile and durable paint. You can use it both indoors and out, combine it with other materials for a flat or glossy surface, and thin it to make a stain.

You can purchase ready-mixed milk paint from mail-order sources, or make your own from these common ingredients:

⅓ cup slaked (hydrated) lime
1 quart milk or buttermilk
¼ cup boiled linseed oil
1½ lbs. whiting or powdered pigments
1 Tbsp. cornstarch

These items are available from a grocery, nursery, paint store, or builder's supply. Because the lime is an alkali, use inert pigments that are unaffected by it. Earth pigments, such as those used to color concrete and cement, work well. You will also find that some pigments are easy to mix and apply; others are less so. To compensate, adjust the ratios of the dry ingredients.

Blend these ingredients, adding pigment until the paint is the consistency of heavy cream. Let the mixture sit for 15 to 30 minutes, mix again, then strain it through a cheesecloth. Milk and oil act as binder and solvent, lime adds body, and pigment adds color. Cornstarch helps to keep the powdered ingredients suspended; even so, it's wise to stir the paint occasionally as you apply it. Use the mixture immediately, and refrigerate it between coats — because of the milk, the paint will not keep for long. Thin the paint with additional milk; clean the brushes with soap and water.

This recipe will give you a flat interior finish. To add gloss, apply the paint, let it dry completely, then cover it with several coats of varnish or linseed oil.

You can purchase natural resins and ready-mixed milk paint from:

Olde Mill Cabinet Shoppe
1660 Camp Betty Washington Road
York, PA 17402

Wood Finishing Supply Company
100 Throop Street
Palmyra, NY 14522

Or, purchase pigments to add to your own milk paints from:

Lee Valley Tools
P.O. Box 6295, Station J
Ottawa, Ontario
K2A 1T4

Johnson Paint Company
355 Newbury Street
Boston, MA 02115

WHICH IS MORE IMPORTANT, ENHANCEMENT OR PROTECTION?

As mentioned in the first chapter, a finish has two purposes — to protect the wood and enhance its beauty. Depending on the project and how it will be used, one of these will take precedence over the other.

For example, when finishing a project that will be used outdoors, you must protect it from the elements above all else. Once you have identified several weatherproof finishes, then you can worry about which of them will look best. If you make a fine piece of furniture that requires a deep, glossy finish, then appearance is paramount; protection is secondary.

Decide how you want your project to appear after it's finished. Also consider how it will be used and in what environment. Furthermore, remember that every finish has certain *properties* that define how it enhances and protects the wood. Depending on the project, one or two properties may take precedence over all the others.

WHAT ENHANCING PROPERTIES DO YOU NEED?

There are several ways that a finish can enhance the beauty of the wood. It does so by altering the appearance of the surface. Decide which of these is the most desirable:

■ *Penetration* — The depth to which a finish penetrates will affect both the looks and the texture of the wood. If it penetrates deeply, it may form only a thin film on the surface, and the natural texture of the wood will be preserved. If allowed to build on the surface, it will replace the natural texture with a smoother one.

■ *Depth* — A *transparent* film builds on the wood to create depth — the visible distance from the surface of the finish to the surface of the wood. The thicker the film, the deeper the finish looks.

FOR YOUR INFORMATION

Depth can also be a protecting property. The thicker the film, the more durable it is likely to be. It may also provide better protection against water and abrupt changes in humidity.

■ *Luster* — A film can either reflect light, bouncing it back at you, or scatter it every which way. A highly reflective film is said to be *glossy*. If the surface scatters the light, it looks dull and *flat*. If it's somewhere in between (both reflective and scattering), it has a *satin* look. (*SEE FIGURE 3-1.*) You can control the luster by using finishes with added *flatteners* (usually powdered quartz), or by rubbing the hardened finish with various abrasives.

3-1 These three pieces of mahogany were all finished with the same brand of polyurethane, but a different amount of flattener was added to the finish on each board. The board on the left has the most flattener, making the finished surface appear *flat*. The board in the middle has only a small amount, just enough to give it a *satin* look. The board on the right has no flattener at all and appears *glossy*.

■ *Tint* — All but a few finishing materials alter the natural color of the wood by tinting the surface. Varnishes, shellacs, and many other transparent finishes have a slightly amber tint which subtly warms up the natural wood tones. (*SEE FIGURE 3-2.*) Stains, dyes, bleaches, and paint can change the color dramatically.

Only waterborne resins and a few other special finishes have no tint. These are said to be *water clear.*

■ *Opacity* — The cloudier the finish looks, the more opaque it is said to be. Opacity depends not only on the resins and oils, but also on the colored pigments, flatteners, and other solids in the film.

3-2 Most transparent finishes are not truly clear — they have a tint that changes the color of the wood. The piece of oak on the top left is unfinished — as you can see, the natural color is very light. The piece of oak on the top right was finished with waterborne acrylic. Of all the transparent finishes, this has the least tint. Spar varnish, shown on the bottom right, has more tint and alters the wood color noticeably. Orange shellac, shown on the bottom left, has a pronounced amber tint and changes the wood color dramatically.

WHAT PROTECTING PROPERTIES DO YOU NEED?

There are also different ways in which a finish can protect the wood. Depending on how the project will be used and under what conditions, some of these will be more important than others:

■ *Hardness* — In comparison to other materials, resinous films are not hard and depend on the wood for most of their strength. However, certain finishes resist wear and tear better than others, and are said to be "harder." Harder finishes are sometimes brittle and prone to chipping. (*SEE FIGURE 3-3.*)

■ *Elasticity* — Films must be flexible and elastic enough to expand and contract as the wood moves. Generally, softer films are more elastic.

■ *Permeability* — A finish should provide a moisture barrier so the wood won't expand or contract too quickly when the humidity changes; quick movements can ruin a project. The lower the permeability, the slower the moisture will pass through the film, and the more stable the wood will be. You can decrease the permeability of most finishes by applying additional coats.

3-3 Polyurethane is extremely hard but can become very brittle, particularly if it's an *interior* polyurethane that has been exposed to sunlight. This is a section of a cedar chest that was finished with interior polyurethane. It sat near a window for several years. When the soft cedar was dented, the finish cracked instead of giving with the wood.

■ *Heat resistance* — Projects may be subjected to high temperatures by spilled hot drinks, steam, and hot pans and serving dishes. The temperature at which a film begins to soften and delaminate determines its heat resistance. (*See Figure 3-4.*)

■ *Water resistance* — Some water-sensitive finishes allow the wood to soak up water; others exclude water but become cloudy when they contact it. Water-resistant finishes will keep their good looks *and* keep water out of the wood, but they won't stand up to constant exposure. (*See Figure 3-5.*) Only finishes that are rated as exterior are truly waterproof.

■ *Chemical resistance* — Finishes vary in their resistance to mildly caustic chemicals in household cleaners, mild acids in fruit and vegetable juices, oils from hands and foods, and alcohol in beer and wine.

■ *Durability* — This is not an individual property, but rather a summing up of all the protective properties. If a finish is hard enough to resist abuse yet elastic enough to move with the wood, *and* resistant to heat, water, and household chemicals, then it's very durable.

FOR YOUR INFORMATION

The same finish can display entirely different properties depending on the species of wood to which it's applied, how the surface is prepared, and how the finish is applied. Remember this when selecting finishes.

3-4 Some finishes tolerate heat better than others. Starting clockwise from the upper left, these four pieces of mahogany were finished with tung oil, waterborne acrylic, lacquer, and polyurethane. A boiling-hot pan was set on all four boards for five minutes, then removed. As you can see, the waterborne resin and lacquer have begun to blister. The tung oil and polyurethane remained intact.

3-5 Finishes differ in their response to water. These pieces of mahogany are finished the same as in *Figure 3-4* — clockwise from the upper left, with tung oil, waterborne acrylic, lacquer, and polyurethane. A cold, wet glass was set on all four boards for one hour, then removed. The grain of the tung-oil board is darkened and the lacquer board has a white ring. The waterborne resin and polyurethane are unaffected.

PROPERTIES OF COMMON FINISHES

ENHANCING PROPERTIES	PROTECTING PROPERTIES

PENETRATION/DEPTH

Penetrating — Drying oils, rubbing oils, dyes, stains

Building — Shellacs, varnishes, polyurethanes, lacquers, waterborne resins, epoxies, oil and latex paints

> *Note: Drying oils and rubbing oils begin to build on the surface after the first or second coat. Most building finishes will penetrate on the first coat if they are thinned with the appropriate solvents.*

LUSTER

Flat — Most penetrating finishes after just one coat. Other finishes can be made to appear flat by adding flatteners or by rubbing them out with the proper abrasives.

Satin — Most penetrating finishes after several coats. Other finishes can take on a satin appearance by adding flatteners or rubbing them out with the proper abrasives.

Glossy — Shellacs, varnishes, polyurethanes, lacquers, waterborne resins, epoxies, oil and latex paints, provided there are no flatteners added. For high gloss, most finishes must be polished after curing.

> *Note: Wax adds gloss to a finish but has no luster of its own.*

TINT

Artificially tinted — Stains, dyes, oil and latex paints. Some varnishes, rubbing oils, and waxes are also tinted.

Natural amber tint — Rubbing oils, drying oils, shellacs, varnishes, polyurethanes, lacquers, epoxies, waxes

Clear (no discernible tint) — Waterborne resins; a very few lacquers, varnishes, and epoxies

OPACITY

Transparent — Rubbing oils, drying oils, shellacs, varnishes, polyurethanes, lacquers, waterborne resins, epoxies, dyes

Semi-transparent — Stains, thinned paints, transparent finishes with added flatteners or pigments, waxes

Opaque — Oil and latex paints

HARDNESS/ELASTICITY

Hard — Epoxies, polyurethanes, varnishes

Moderately hard — Lacquers, waterborne resins, oil and latex paints

Moderately elastic — Rubbing oils, shellacs (although shellacs become less elastic with time)

Elastic — Drying oils, stains, dyes, waxes

PERMEABILITY

Impermeable — Paraffin wax

Semi-permeable — Other waxes, shellacs, varnishes, polyurethanes, epoxies, oil paints

Permeable — Drying oils, rubbing oils, lacquers, waterborne resins, latex paints, stains, dyes

HEAT RESISTANCE

High heat resistance — Polyurethanes, epoxies, oils paints

Moderate heat resistance — Rubbing oils, lacquers, varnishes, waterborne resins, latex paints

Low heat resistance — Drying oils, shellacs

WATER RESISTANCE

Water-sensitive — Drying oils, some rubbing oils, shellacs, lacquers

Water-resistant — Some rubbing oils, waterborne resins, interior varnishes, polyurethanes, latex and oil paints

Waterproof — Exterior varnishes, polyurethanes, waterborne resins, latex and oil paints, epoxies

CHEMICAL RESISTANCE

Chemically sensitive — Drying oils, shellacs, waxes

Chemically resistant — Rubbing oils, lacquers, waterborne resins, latex paints

Highly chemically resistant — Varnishes, polyurethanes, epoxies, oil paints

DURABILITY

Highly durable — Varnishes, polyurethanes, epoxies, oil paints, dyes

Moderately durable — Shellac, lacquers, waterborne resins, latex paints, stains

Not very durable — Drying oils, rubbing oils, waxes

MISCELLANEOUS PROPERTIES

TOXICITY

Highly toxic — Epoxies, as well as some varnishes, paints, and rubbing oils

Moderately toxic — Lacquers, some varnishes, polyurethanes, some oil and latex paints, some stains, dyes

Moderately safe — Some drying oils, some rubbing oils, shellacs, some waterborne resins, some stains, some waxes

Nontoxic — Some drying and rubbing oils, some waterborne resins, some paints, some waxes

METHODS OF APPLICATION

Wipe-on — Drying oils, rubbing oils, stains, dyes, waxes

Pour-on — Epoxies

Brush-on — Shellacs, some lacquers, varnishes, polyurethanes, some waterborne resins, oil and latex paints

Spray-on — Some lacquers, some waterborne resins

> *Note: Not every specific finish will fit the neat pigeonholes in this chart. Depending on its ingredients, a particular brand of finish may display completely different properties from the norm. The information here should be taken as a general guide; there is not sufficient room to cover all the exceptions.*

HOW MUCH TIME AND WHAT EQUIPMENT ARE NEEDED TO APPLY A FINISH?

It's not enough to know that a certain finish can be made to produce a certain effect. You must know *how* to achieve that effect, and whether you have the time and the equipment to do it.

For example, both shellac and lacquer will build to a deep finish, provided you apply several coats. Shellac is usually brushed on and must dry for an hour or more between coats. Furthermore, it requires a light sanding between coats and thorough rubbing after the last coat keep the film even and to polish it to the desired luster. Lacquer, on the other hand, is usually sprayed on, requires less time between coats, and needs little rub-out. Consequently, you can build depth with lacquer much more quickly than you can with shellac. But lacquer also requires a spray gun, a respirator, and a ventilated spray booth.

In short, shellac takes more time, while lacquer involves more equipment. If you require a deep finish and time is not a problem, choose shellac. But if time is short and you can afford the necessary equipment, select lacquer. To help decide whether you have the time or equipment to apply a particular finish, consider its normal method of application. Don't attempt a finish that stretches your resources.

TESTING THE POSSIBILITIES

Whether you narrow your choices to several possible finishes or just one, you will want to experiment *before* you apply any finish to your project. This is especially important if you've never used a finish before, never applied it to a particular species of wood, or never used a particular method of application.

Select a scrap large enough to make a test board. This board must be the same species as the wood your project is built from. Its size will depend on how many finishes you have to test. Ideally, you should test them all on the same board — this makes it easier to compare the results. (*SEE FIGURE 3-6.*)

Prepare the surface of the test board just as you would the project. *This is extremely important!* If you don't scrape, sand, and fill the wood exactly as you will your project, then the test results may be misleading. If you are unsure as to how to prepare the surface, make it part of your test — prepare different areas of the board in different ways.

Before you start, label which areas you will cover with what finishes. You may also wish to test different methods of application and varying numbers of finish coats. Apply each finish to its designated area, masking off the other areas to prevent contamination.

In some cases, you may want to apply the possible finishes in a grid so you can see how various combinations of chemicals react. For example, suppose you have chosen several stains *and* several building finishes to apply over those stains. Prepare the surface of the test board, then apply the various stains in long, horizontal stripes. Let the stains dry completely, and apply the finishes in vertical stripes. Where the stripes cross, you'll be able to see which combinations you like best. You'll also be able to tell if any of the stains and finishes you've picked are incompatible. (*SEE FIGURE 3-7.*)

I cannot overemphasize the importance of this test board, *especially* if you have no experience with a particular finish or finishing method. The test board not only helps you choose between different finishes, it lets you practice with new chemicals and techniques before using them on a project. It's much better to find that a particular combination of finishing chemicals is incompatible on a test board than on the real thing.

> ## TRY THIS TRICK
>
> **K**eep your test boards for future reference. To save space, cut 6-inch squares from the boards and resaw them to ¼ inch thick. Fill out an index card for each square, describing how you produced the finish, and glue the card to the back. I file my squares in a "finish file" — a cardboard box that I keep on top of the finishing cabinet.

Once you've completed the tests, examine the results carefully. If aesthetics are most important, pick the finish that looks best to you. If protection is more critical than appearance, you may want to conduct additional tests by applying water, heat, sharp objects, small children, and other types of abuse to the test board before making a final choice.

> ## TRY THIS TRICK
>
> **T**here is no rule that says you must apply the same finish to the entire project. Sometimes, it's best not to do so. Old-time cabinetmakers frequently applied a protective finish to the tabletops and chair seats (where it was most needed), and a decorative finish to the legs, aprons, and rungs.

3-6 This test strip was made prior to finishing the "Step-Back Cupboard" in the *Projects* section. I wanted to use an old-time milk paint finish, one color over another. I tried several color combinations on this piece of poplar. Red over yellow produced the most pleasing effect, followed by green over red.

3-7 This test board was used to try several possible stain and finish combinations for the "Miniature Mule Chest" on page 92 of the *Projects* section. I glued up scraps of cherry to make a board wide enough to do a grid, then applied several stains and dyes in horizontal stripes and clear finishes in vertical stripes. Note that not all of the finishes bonded properly to some of the stains. The combination that I liked best was a water-based aniline dye covered with lacquer.

MIXING BRANDS: RARELY A GOOD IDEA

More and more, finish manufacturers are offering wood finishing *systems* — stains, fillers, sealers, primers, coatings, thinners — everything you need to finish a project. This is especially common with spray-on lacquers and waterborne resins — both of which are chemically complex. All the materials within a system are formulated to be compatible with one another — you needn't worry that a stain or a sealer will prevent the coating from bonding or drying properly.

Often, the same is true within a certain *brand* of materials, even though the manufacturer may not advertise it as a system. It would confuse the customer needlessly to offer incompatible finishes under the same brand name. For this reason alone, it's a good idea not to mix brands, if you can avoid it.

There are other reasons, too. Reputable manufacturers warrant their products; by mixing brands, you often void the warranties on all the materials. If you're using a system, the various components may be necessary to one another to form a durable finish. If you make a substitution, your final finish may lack a key ingredient.

Test strips, while extremely important, don't always tell the whole story. You may be able to produce a pleasing finish, but how durable is it? Will it hold its color and luster? Will it continue to look just as good after it sees some wear and tear? You can be reasonably certain that it will if you haven't mixed brands, since most manufacturers test their products for such things. But if you have, then the finish on your project will be an experiment.

4

PREPARING THE SURFACE

Woodworking can be hard on wood, particularly the *surface* of the wood. During the course of a project, you assault the surface time and time again. Power tools tear the wood grain, creating ridges and mill marks; hand tools make dents, scratches, and gouges; assembly and constant handling leave dirt, oil, and glue spots.

Any one of these surface flaws could ruin a finish. Mill marks and glue spots will cause a wood stain to appear blotchy or uneven; dents and scratches interrupt the smooth appearance and luster of a film; oil and dirt may prevent the film from bonding properly with the wood. When it comes time to finish a project, you must undo all the damage that you've done.

Furthermore, depending on the finish you have selected, you must prepare the surface of the wood in a particular manner. You must sand to the proper grit and clean the surface in the proper manner. If the surface is poorly or improperly prepared, it may diminish the enhancing or protective properties of the finish.

INSPECTING THE SURFACE

KNOWING WHAT TO LOOK FOR

Many of the surface flaws that can ruin a finish are not easily recognizable. To know what to look for, you must understand how wood absorbs a finish, and how the finish changes its appearance.

Every piece of wood has two types of grain, and they absorb the finish in different ways. Depending on the grain pattern of the wood and how a board is cut, a wood surface will show *end grain, long grain,* or both. End grain is cut across the wood fibers, while long grain is parallel to them. In addition, there are light and dark bands running through the wood, commonly called the annual rings. Actually, the light bands are *springwood,* and the dark bands *summerwood.* Springwood grows rapidly early in the year, and is much softer and less dense than the slow-growing summerwood that forms later in the season. End grain and springwood absorb finish faster and soak up more of it than long grain and summerwood. (*SEE FIGURE 4-1.*)

As wood absorbs a finish, the optical properties change according to the nature of the finish. Clear finishes make the wood more translucent; stains and dyes change its color. The more finish the wood absorbs, the more pronounced this change becomes. This is why a finish seems to bring out the grain when you apply it. Because springwood absorbs more finish than summerwood, the contrast between them is heightened.

The same is true of end grain and long grain, but here the change is much more pronounced because end grain absorbs so much more finish than long grain. This is what makes curly wood, bird's-eye, burls, and other figured grain look so spectacular when you apply a finish. Because the grain travels in waves or swirls through the wood, the surfaces that would ordinarily show just long grain reveal end grain as well. (*SEE FIGURE 4-2.*)

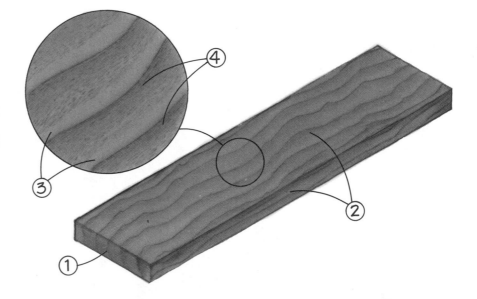

4-1 Some parts of the wood will soak up more finish than others. *End grain* (1) absorbs more finish than *long grain* (2). Also, the light-colored bands of *springwood* (3) absorb more finish than *summerwood* (4). Because a finish changes the appearance of the wood, end grain and springwood will change more than long grain and summerwood.

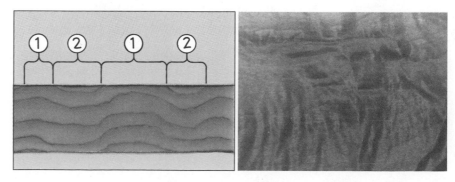

4-2 Wood with a curly grain figure shows both *long grain* (1) and *end grain* (2) on its face. Because end grain absorbs more finish than long grain, a finish emphasizes the wood figure, making the different grains stand out from one another.

This phenomenon can cause a finish to detract from the beauty of the wood grain just as easily as it can enhance it. When you stain a tabletop, the ends will absorb more stain than the faces and sides and appear much too dark in comparison. Because of the way wood is sliced from a log to make plywood, the bands of springwood and summerwood are unnaturally broad. This makes a finish — especially a tinted finish or a stain — look uneven. The rotary cutters of planers, jointers, and routers all leave little ridges on the surface of the wood. The peaks and the valleys show long grain, while the slopes show end grain. A finish heightens the contrast between these areas, just as it does on figured wood. *(SEE FIGURE 4-3.)* Scratches, splits, and cracks also reveal end grain where the eye expects only long grain, and a finish makes these flaws stand out.

Difference in wood grain is not the only thing that can cause the uneven absorption of finish. Excess glue will soak into the wood and prevent it from absorbing a finish or stain. So will wax and oil. If you attempt to finish over these substances, the contaminated area will appear a different color or shade than the rest of the wood surface. In addition, wax and oil may prevent a finish from bonding or curing properly. This is a common problem with water-based varnishes and lacquers.

A finish may also emphasize dents, gouges, and gaps in the wood or joinery. If these flaws are extremely small, the finish may fill them in and hide them from view. More likely, if they're big enough to see, they're too big for the finish to fill. They will instead become more noticeable as voids and depressions in the finished surface.

In short, a finish will actually *magnify* the surface flaws. If you don't find these flaws and eliminate them, the finish will have exactly the opposite effect that you want — it will make the project look worse instead of better.

FINDING THE FLAWS

To avoid this disappointment, you must closely inspect the surface *continually* as you prepare it for a finish. Look at it from several different angles *under a bright, oblique light.* The viewing angles and the bright light are extremely important! *(SEE FIGURE 4-4.)* This is the only way you can find mill marks, small dents, shallow scratches, and other tiny defects.

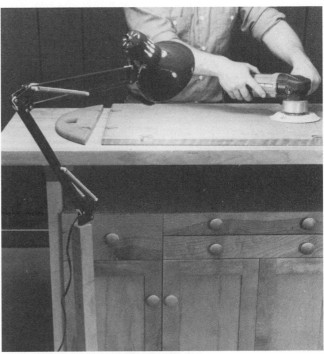

4-4 Many experienced craftsmen consider an adjustable inspection light to be the most valuable finishing tool in their shop. Only by shining a bright light obliquely across a surface, then viewing it from several different angles, can you discover all the tiny flaws and defects.

4-3 Rotary cutters and knives, such as those found on planers, jointers, and routers, all leave *mill marks* (1) — tiny ridges in the wood. These mill marks show both *end grain* (2) and *long grain* (3). Because end grain absorbs more finish than long grain, a finish will make the mill marks stand out. Because mill marks are hard to see before you apply a finish, they are perhaps the most commonly overlooked surface flaws.

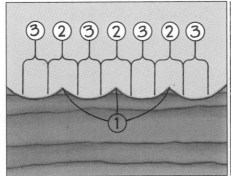

You must also feel for those defects that you cannot easily see. Unfortunately, your hands will deposit oils on the wood if you constantly rub them over the surface. Instead, keep an old piece of nylon stocking handy. As you scrape and sand, wipe the nylon cloth over the wood every so often. If there are any defects, it will snag on them.

For Best Results

Inspect the parts of a project and eliminate as many of the flaws as possible *before* assembly. It's much easier to inspect and smooth surfaces of single boards or simple subassemblies than it is completed projects. You should, in fact, start preparing the wood surface for a finish when you begin the project and continue as you build the project up. In that way, when the project is complete, all the surfaces should be fairly smooth.

SMOOTHING THE SURFACE

MAKING REPAIRS

Once you have begun to identify the flaws on the surface, smooth them over. Start with the biggest and most noticeable defects — dents, gouges, chips, and cracks. All of these must be fixed by repairing the wood surface. You must glue the fractured wood together, splice in new wood, or swell the existing wood. (*SEE FIGURES 4-5 THROUGH 4-10.*)

Some large defects, such as nail holes or poorly fitted joints, must be filled with wood putty or stick shellac. (*SEE FIGURE 4-11.*) These materials will not absorb stain or finish, so their color can't be changed once you apply them. You must choose the proper shade of putty or shellac, or color the putty with dyes or artist's oils before you apply it. For this reason, some craftsmen prefer to wait until *after* the wood surface has been stained, filled, and sealed to fix these flaws. It's much easier to match the color at that time.

ADJUSTABLE INSPECTION LAMP

You must inspect the wood surface constantly: not only when you're preparing the surface for a finish, but throughout the finishing process. Overhead lights do not provide adequate illumination for proper inspection — the light is too diffuse and too far away from the project. Instead, you need a bright (60 to 100 watt) inspection lamp that you can adjust to shine *across* the surface of the wood at a variety of angles.

One of the best inspection lamps (and one of the least expensive) is a low-cost tension lamp mounted on a lightweight floor stand. You can easily move the lamp wherever you need it and quickly change the height or the direction of the light.

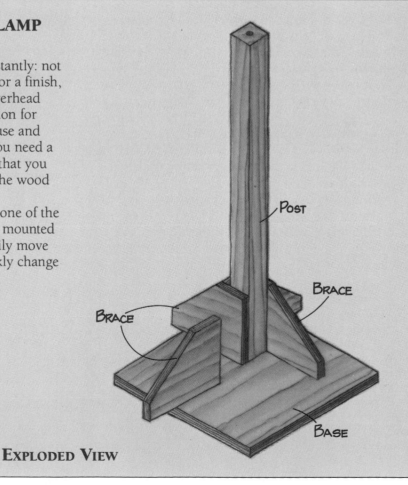

POST

BRACE

BRACE

BASE

EXPLODED VIEW

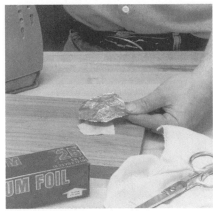

4-5 To eliminate a dent, you must swell the crushed fibers back to their original condition. Cut a piece of clean cloth slightly larger than the dent, soak it in water, and place it over the dent. Place a piece of aluminum foil over the cloth — this seals the water in.

4-6 Heat up a laundry iron as hot as it will go, then press it against the foil. Leave it there long enough for the water in the cloth to turn to steam, but not long enough to scorch the wood. The steam will penetrate the crushed wood fibers and swell them back to their original shape, eliminating the dent. For deep dents or dents in hard wood, moisten the cloth again and repeat this process several times.

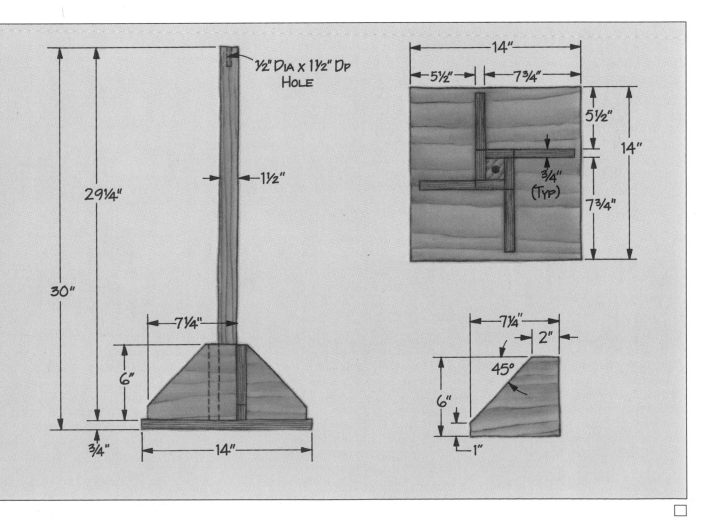

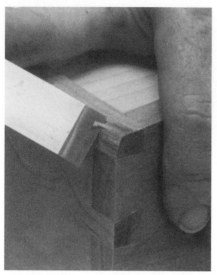

4-7   If the surface is badly gouged or chipped, you may have to splice a small piece of wood onto the damaged area. First, flatten the rough, split-out surface with a small chisel to create a level gluing surface.

4-8   Inspect the leftover scraps from your project to find one whose grain matches the color and texture of the damaged area. From this, cut a small block or wedge slightly larger than you need. Glue it to the surface you have prepared, carefully aligning the grain direction.

4-9   Let the glue dry completely, then file or sand the splice flush with the surface of the surrounding wood. If the color, texture, and grain direction of the splice match the surrounding wood surface, the repair should be almost invisible.

4-10   To repair wood that has cracked or split, glue the pieces back together. If you must force glue into a narrow space, put a dab of glue into the middle of a folded piece of paper and insert the edge of the paper in the crack. Using your fingers as if you were forcing tooth-paste from a tube, squeeze the glue along the paper and into the crack.

4-11   One of the quickest ways to fill small gaps or voids in the wood surface is with *stick shellac*. This material comes in dozens of colors. Select the one that most closely matches the color of the *finished* wood, using your test strip as a reference. Heat an old, blunt knife with an alcohol lamp or propane torch, then carve a small amount of shellac

from the stick with the hot tip. Continue to use the knife to melt the material into the void. If the knife cools before you can completely fill the defect, heat it up again. The shellac is ready to sand smooth as soon as it cools.

However, putty and shellac must be sanded flush with the surrounding surface once they've cured or cooled. If you have already applied some finishing materials, you might sand through them, expose raw wood, and alter the color around the defect. You'll have to make "spot repairs," reapplying and blending stains, fillers, or sealers in these areas, hoping to get the same shade that you had before. To avoid this hassle, most woodworkers opt to fill the defect before they start sanding.

Tint the wood putty or select a stick of shellac to match the finish color on your test strip. (If you haven't made a test strip, do so. Or, refer to a previous project that you built from the same wood and finished with the same materials.) When you're satisfied with the color, apply the putty or shellac to the wood. Let the patching material harden and sand it flush.

PLANING AND SCRAPING

If the surface is especially rough or badly scratched, smooth the surface with a *hand plane. (SEE FIGURES 4-12 AND 4-13.)* When the wood is in bad shape, planes have advantages over many other surfacing tools, including power sanders. With a little practice, you can smooth the surface of a rough board much faster than you can with a belt sander. If the plane iron is sharp and properly adjusted, the plane will not leave scratches like a sander. And because the sole of the

plane prevents you from cutting much deeper than the surrounding wood, you cannot dwell on just the damaged area — you have to plane the surface all around it. This keeps you from creating dips and depressions in the surface.

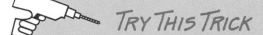

TRY THIS TRICK

To prevent chipped and torn grain when surfacing figured lumber, plane the lumber to within $1/16$ inch of its final thickness with a planer. Then work the boards down to size with a razor-sharp jointer plane.

If the wood surface is reasonably flat, with nothing worse than mill marks or a few shallow scratches, smooth the surface with a *scraper*. This hand tool removes a tiny amount of wood with each stroke, much less than a hand plane. Nonetheless, scrapers are much faster to use than most power sanders, and more economical than all of them.

A scraper is a thin sheet of tool steel with a small burr on the edge. As you push the scraper across the wood, the burr acts as a tiny plane iron, shearing off a layer of wood so thin that you can see through it. *(SEE FIGURES 4-14 AND 4-15.)* This burr is more versatile than a plane iron. You can cut in any direction and at any

4-12 Smooth large, rough, or damaged surfaces with a jack plane or jointer plane (shown). Adjust the plane iron to remove a paper-thin layer of wood all the way across the cutting edge. Use long, slow strokes, keeping the iron at a slight angle to the grain direction.

4-13 For small areas and end grain, use a block plane. Again, adjust the plane iron to take the thinnest shavings possible, and cut from the outside of the board in toward the center. A *low-angle* block plane (shown) works best for hardwood end grains.

angle to the wood grain, pushing the scraper away or pulling it toward you. You can also control the degree of smoothness with which a scraper cuts by altering the size of the burr. (See "Sharpening a Scraper" on page 40.) The smaller the burr, the smoother the cut.

FOR YOUR INFORMATION

Hand planes and scrapers don't get used up, they don't produce fine dust, and they cut faster than sandpaper. To save time, money, and your good health, plane and scrape as much as possible. Use sanders and sandpaper just in the final stages of smoothing the wood surface.

SANDING

Even though you can create an extremely smooth surface with planing and scraping, you must do *some* sanding to properly prepare the wood for a finish. Both planing and scraping mash the wood fibers, clos-

4-14 To use a scraper, tilt it in the same direction as the cut. Experiment with this tilt angle until you feel the tool bite into the wood and peel off a thin shaving. Some craftsmen use their thumbs to flex the thin steel slightly; this lifts the corners off the wood so they will not scratch the surface. Also, angle the scraper edge so it's not quite perpendicular to the direction in which you're pushing or pulling it. This keeps the scraper from following ridges and dips, and the tool cuts a flatter surface.

ing the pores. Sanding opens them up again, helping the finish to penetrate. It also creates tiny, invisible scratches in the surface, which gives a non-penetrating finish something to hold on to, and increases the strength of the bond between the finish and the wood. (*SEE FIGURE 4-16.*)

There are two ways to sand a project — by hand and with machines. When sanding by hand, use a sanding block to distribute pressure over a large area and speed the work. (*SEE FIGURE 4-17.*) The block also performs the same function as the sole of a plane, preventing you from dwelling in one tiny area and sanding a dip or depression in the surface. Because most wooden surfaces are flat, sanding blocks are normally rectangular with flat faces. But if the surface to be sanded is contoured, the block should mirror its shape.

When sanding by machine, you have a choice of several tools. The *random orbital sander* is, perhaps, the best multipurpose sander — it removes stock quickly, smooths large and medium-size areas, and performs both rough and fine sanding chores. However, you may also need a *belt sander* for large areas and rough work, an *orbital sander* for smaller areas and fine work, a *drum sander* for sanding contours, and a *flap sander* for smoothing three-dimensional shapes. (*SEE FIGURE 4-18.*)

4-15 Scrapers come in several sizes and shapes. Choose the one that best fits the surface you must smooth. You can also find scrapers of several thicknesses. The thinner the scraper, the smaller the burr on the edge and the smoother the scraper will cut.

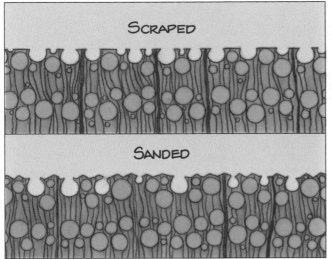

4-16 Planing and scraping cut or shear the wood, leaving a flat surface. Sanding scratches it, creating ridges and valleys. If the sandpaper grit is small enough, these scratches will be too small to be seen. Nonetheless, even small scratches increase the surface area and present the finish with more wood to hold on to. This strengthens the mechanical bond between the wood and the finish.

4-17 To speed the work and produce better results when hand sanding, wrap the sandpaper around a *sanding block*. This block must be small enough to fit your hand comfortably, and its surface should be firm but resilient. You can purchase commercial sanding blocks made of cork or rubber, or you can make your own by gluing several layers of felt to a block of wood.

4-18 There are many different hand-held power sanding tools to choose from, but you can perform most sanding chores with the five shown here. Many craftsmen prefer the *random orbital sander* (1) for most jobs — it can be used for every-

thing from quick stock removal to fine sanding. A palm sander or *orbital sander* (2) is designed for small tasks and fine work, while a *belt sander* (3) is the traditional choice for large sanding jobs. The *drum sander* (4) is not a power tool in its own right, but

a curve-sanding attachment for a power drill or drill press. The *flap sander* (5) is another drill attachment that enables you to sand three-dimensional shapes.

SHARPENING A SCRAPER

If there is a disadvantage to using a scraper, it's that it requires frequent sharpening. The burrs on the cutting edges wear out quickly, particularly when you're scraping hardwood. The shavings from each cutting stroke grow progressively smaller until they're no bigger than sawdust. At this point, you must put new cutting edges on a scraper. There are two ways to do this — the traditional way and the quick way.

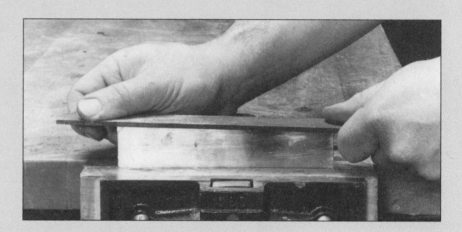

1 **To sharpen a scraper in the** traditional manner, first make the edges straight and flat with a smooth-cut file. If the scraper is in good shape, this should only take a few strokes of the file.

2 **Remove the old burrs from** the arrises (where the faces and edges meet) with a sharpening stone, whetting both faces of the scraper. Keep each face flat on the stone as you rub it in a circular motion. The burrs will disappear in a few seconds.

3 **Polish the edges on the** sharpening stone, holding the scraper square to the stone's surface. This will create square, sharp arrises.

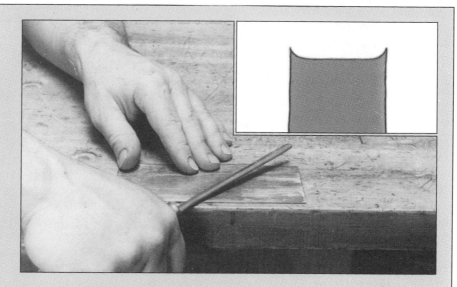

4 **To raise the burrs, hold** the scraper with one face flat on the workbench and run a *burnisher* along the long arrises, pressing down hard. (A burnisher is a round or oval-shaped length of tempered steel.) Hold the burnisher almost, but not quite, parallel to the face of the scraper. Repeat for the opposite face.

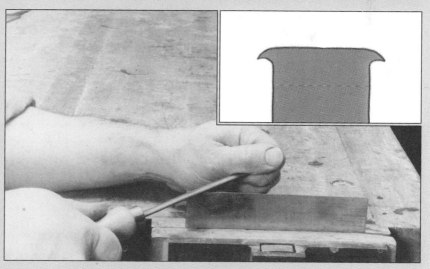

5 **To turn the burrs so they** can be used to cut the wood, clamp the scraper in a vise with one edge facing up. Run the burnisher along an arris, holding it almost, but not quite, perpendicular to the face. Repeat for each arris. **Note:** The pressure used to raise and turn the burrs will control the size of the burrs. The greater the pressure, the larger the burr.

6 **To sharpen a scraper quickly,** remove the old burrs by rubbing the faces on a sharpening stone. Then file the edge flat with a *single-cut mill file.* The filing will create a sharp, clean-cutting burr on one arris. If you wish, clamp the file in a vise while you're working. Then all you have to do to touch up a scraper's cutting edge is pass it over the file a few times. The disadvantages to this system are that it does not create a usable burr on all arrises, and you cannot easily control the size of the burr.

In addition to a selection of sanding tools, you also have a choice of *abrasives*. There are four types of sandpaper commonly available, two of which are useful in preparing a wood surface for a finish:

■ *Flint* is made from ground quartz, is white or cream-colored, and does not cut well or stay sharp for very long. But it's very inexpensive, which makes it a good choice for rough work that requires lots of sandpaper. However, do not use it when preparing a surface for a fine finish.

■ *Garnet* is also a natural abrasive, appears red or pink, and is favored by most craftsmen for hand sanding. The cutting edges of the garnet grains won't endure the punishment of power sanding, but they will last a long time when used for lighter tasks. Furthermore, garnet never dulls. As you use the sandpaper, the grains fracture now and then, constantly exposing new cutting edges. The paper continues to cut well until it loads up with sawdust or the garnet wears off.

■ *Aluminum oxide* is a synthetic abrasive, tan or brown in color, and is best used for power sanding. The grains are extremely hard and stand up well to the high pressures and speeds generated by a revolving belt or disk. Unlike garnet, however, they do grow dull.

■ *Silicon carbide* is also a synthetic, and is available in black (wet/dry) and white (dry only). It's much harder than other abrasives, but not particularly durable or well suited for sanding raw wood. Instead, this is the best choice for sanding *coated* surfaces — smoothing the finish in preparation for additional coats or rubbing out the final finish.

No matter what sanding tool or abrasive you use, work your way up through the grit numbers as you sand, proceeding from coarse to smooth *without skipping any grits*. Sandpaper scratches the wood surface as it cuts, and by progressing through the grits, you continually trade one set of scratches for a smaller set until the scratches become too small to see. If you skip grits, it's much harder to erase the large scratches with small ones — in all probability, you'll leave a few large scratches behind. These will stand out when you apply a finish.

However, don't begin with extremely coarse sandpaper. Grits below 100 (medium) are generally intended for removing stock and shaping wood rather than smoothing its surface. Furthermore, planing and scraping leave a surface smoother than you could sand it with 100-grit paper. A coarse grit might make the wood rougher rather than smoother. In most cases, it's best to start with 100- or 120-grit.

TRY THIS TRICK

How do you know when to move up to the next grit? Use your inspection light to study the *scratch pattern* — the ridges left by the abrasive. If these are relatively even, it's time to move up to a finer grit. If there appear to be large scratches mixed with smaller ones, continue sanding with the same grit.

Where do you stop? That depends on the finish you want to apply and the properties you want it to display. In general, the appearance of most *building* finishes — shellac, lacquer, varnish, waterborne resin, etc. — are unaffected by how smooth you sand the surface, provided you remove all the visible scratches and other defects. The liquid finish flows over the wood surface, filling in microscopic irregularities. When hardened, the finish displays its own distinctive surface, no matter what's underneath it. Beyond a certain grit, sanding the surface smoother is wasted effort.

A supersmooth surface may, in fact, have an adverse effect on a building finish. As mentioned previously, finishes form mechanical bonds with the wood. The smoother the surface, the weaker these bonds are. For these reasons, it's best to stop sanding at 150- or 180- (medium-fine) grit. At this stage, all the scratches are invisible, yet the surface remains rough enough for the finish to adhere properly.

These considerations change when you apply a *penetrating* finish such as tung oil or Danish oil. Because these films are so thin, the wood surface directly affects the luster. The smoother you sand the wood — especially closed-grain hardwoods — the glossier the final finish will look. And because these chemicals penetrate the wood, a smooth surface does not inhibit the bond between the wood and the finish film. If you want a flat look, you can still stop at 150- or 180-grit. The film begins to show some gloss when the wood has been sanded to 220- (fine) grit, and this gloss continues to increase up to 320- or 400- (very fine) grit.

If you intend to apply a *stain* underneath the finish, particularly a pigmented oil stain, there are still other considerations. The pigment is a solid powder that collects in the pores and minute scratches on the wood surface. The deeper the scratches, the more pigment collects in them, and the darker the stain looks. Smooth surfaces with shallow scratches collect less pigment, and the stain appears lighter. (*SEE FIGURE*

4-19.) In short, you can control the shade of the stain by how smooth you sand the project. Of course, you must sand until the sanding scratches are too small to see — 150- or 180-grit — but how far you go beyond that depends on the color you want to achieve. You may have to experiment with a few test pieces before you can decide which grit to end with.

Here are a few additional sanding tips:

■ Refold the sandpaper or shift it on the sanding block every so often to expose fresh cutting surfaces.

■ Rotate the sandpaper one quarter turn every minute or so to prevent the sawdust from clogging the sandpaper. When the sandpaper becomes loaded with dust, it will no longer cut.

■ Constantly vacuum up or brush away the saw-dust as you sand. This, too, will keep the dust from loading the sandpaper.

■ After finishing with one grit, vacuum the surface before sanding with a finer grit. This will remove any of the abrasives that may have come loose from the coarser sandpaper.

■ If you intend to apply a waterborne resin finish, avoid "non-loading" papers. These are coated with a special wax to keep the sawdust from sticking to them. That wax may contaminate the wood surface and prevent the water-based finish from bonding properly.

■ If loading is a problem, try "open-coat" abrasives. On open-coat sandpaper, only 40 to 70 percent of the surface is coated with grit. Consequently, the sawdust doesn't become wedged between the cutting edges.

■ Sand in a straight line, using long, even strokes. This will create an even scratch pattern.

■ Stick to a plan, sanding all the surfaces evenly; don't just sand until the wood feels smooth. Repeat the plan with each grit.

■ Be careful not to round-over edges that you want to remain crisp or adjoining surfaces that will be glued together. If there is an area of the wood you don't want to sand for some reason, protect it with masking tape.

■ When the sandpaper loses its bite, discard it and get a fresh piece. Don't overuse a sheet of sandpaper. When the grit wears off, there's nothing left but the glue and sizing that held that grit on the paper. If you continue to use the paper, you'll be rubbing these materials into the wood. This, in turn, may interfere with the finish.

■ Do your final sanding right before you apply a finish. If you wait too long between the final sanding and applying the finish, the surface may be contaminated with dust, dirt, or grime — and you'll have to perform the final sanding all over again.

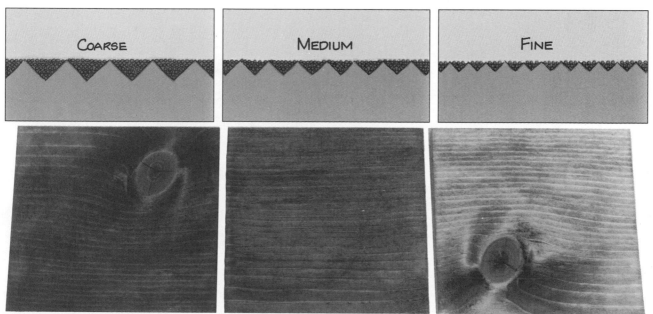

4-19 When you apply an oil stain to a surface that has been sanded with coarse sandpaper, a lot of pig-ment collects in the deep scratches and the stain looks very dark. Finer sandpaper leaves shallower scratches, less pigment collects in them, and the stain appears lighter. These three boards were sanded to 100-grit, 150-grit, and 220-grit, from left to right. The same stain was applied to all three, yet each appears to be a dif-ferent shade. By carefully choosing the grit that you sand to, you can control the shade of the stain.

RAISING THE GRAIN

Many of the things you do to the wood as you build a project — planing, jointing, sawing, routing — mash or crush the wood fibers. Those fibers nearest the surface of the wood are usually the ones in the worst shape. Yet these are the very fibers you want to be open and receptive when you apply the finish.

To help restore the wood fibers near the surface, *raise the grain* before you do your final sanding. Use a clean cloth or brush to wet the surface with water. Contrary to popular belief, this will not hurt the wood — wood, after all, is partly made from water. It will cause the wood fibers near the surface to swell back to their original shape before they were beaten down. (*SEE FIGURE 4-20.*) The wood will look and feel rough, but the raised grain can be easily sanded smooth. In the process, you'll open many more pores to receive the finish.

Raising the grain will also cause severed fibers or *whiskers* to stand up so you can easily sand them off. Whiskers are especially common on open-grain woods such as oak and mahogany. If you don't get rid of the whiskers before you apply a finish, they may stand up afterward. They are much harder to get rid of after you begin to apply the finish, and can cause a great deal of mischief depending on the finish you want to apply.

Although raising the grain is always a good idea, it's not absolutely necessary before applying solvent-based finishes. However, it's essential if you will use a grain-raising finishing material such as a water-soluble aniline dye or waterborne resins. To ensure that the wood remains smooth and needs only minimal sanding after you apply these products, you *must* raise the grain and sand it down again beforehand. Otherwise, you'll need to sand the wood after the dye or finish dries. This is counterproductive, since you must sand off the material you just applied to the wood.

CLEANING THE SURFACE
FINAL PREPARATIONS

Cleaning is one of the most important steps in preparing the surface, and one of the most often overlooked. Many woodworkers presume that, because they have removed a layer of wood by scraping and sanding, the surface is now clean. This is not necessarily so.

Even though you've brushed or vacuumed away the sawdust as you sanded, much of it — some of it too small to see — remains on the wood surface. If you don't remove the fine dust, it will mix with the finish, clouding the film or ruining the luster.

FOR YOUR INFORMATION

A sanding sealer will also make the whiskers stand up so they can be sanded off.

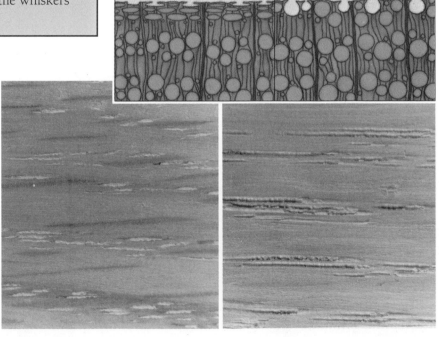

4-20 Woodworking processes often mash the fibers on the surface of the wood, as shown on the left. This closes the wood pores, prevents the finish from penetrating, and may interfere with the bond between the finish and the wood surface. To restore the crushed fibers, wet the wood and let it dry completely prior to the final sanding. The damaged fibers will swell, raising the grain, as shown on the right. Afterward, you can sand the raised grain smooth again.

FOR BEST RESULTS

Before you can properly clean a project, you should clean your shop — or at least clean the finishing area. If you don't, you'll stir up the dust and dirt as you walk around and it will resettle on your clean project. Furthermore, if you apply a finish without cleaning your shop, this dust could settle on the wet chemical film and become imbedded in it.

To begin the final cleaning, brush off the project thoroughly with a stiff bristle brush, then vacuum the wood surface. But don't stop there — even careful brushing and vacuuming doesn't remove all the sawdust. You should also rub the surface down with a *tack rag,* a clean cloth impregnated with a substance to make the dust stick to it. You can purchase ready-to-use tack rags, but you must be careful when using them. These are made with waxes and other chemi-

cals that are incompatible with some finishes, particularly waterborne resins. If you rub too hard or too much with the rag, you could contaminate the surface with these chemicals and ruin the finish.

It's much safer to make your own tack rags. Simply sprinkle a little of the finish you intend to use on a piece of cheesecloth and work it in. Within a few minutes, the cloth will feel slightly tacky. Rub it lightly over the surface, picking up the fine dust. If the rag loses its tack, work a little more finish into it. Store the cloth in a plastic bag, labeled so you know what finish has been worked into the fabric. You can use the cloth again to clean another surface prior to applying the *same finish.* But if you plan to apply something different, prepare another cloth.

If you suspect that a surface may be contaminated with wax or oil, wipe it down with naphtha. This solvent will dissolve most oils and waxes, but it doesn't raise the grain or leave any residue behind as it evaporates.

BENCH-MOUNTED SHAVE HORSE

When you scrape or sand a board, you must clamp it to or brace it on the workbench. If you have a lot of boards to smooth, the continual clamping and unclamping becomes tedious. To eliminate this tedium and speed the smoothing chore, old-time craftsmen often used a *shave horse* — a specialized workbench with a foot-operated clamp.

Most shave horses were large affairs, at least as large as an ordinary workbench. However, you can build a smaller version that mounts to your workbench. The bench-mounted shave horse shown can be adapted to almost any bench, and will hold both small and medium-size workpieces while you scrape or sand them.

To adapt this jig to your workbench, first adjust the length of the mounts. When attached to the workbench, these mounts should stretch from the shave horse table almost (but not quite) to the opposite side of the workbench top. Also adjust both the thickness of the table spacers to hold the table at the same level as the workbench, and the width of the trim to match the thickness of the workbench top.

Make the table, knee rest, and footrest from ply-

wood, and the remaining parts from solid wood. Cut the parts to size, mitering or beveling edges where shown in the drawings. Note that the front end of each knee rest mount has two small 10-degree miters, as shown in the *Knee Rest Mount Layout.* These act as stops, preventing the knee rest from pivoting more than 10 degrees up or down. Round-over the bottom edge of the clamp, as shown in the *Side View.*

Drill the mounting holes and pivot holes in the table, beam, mounts, knee rest braces, knee rest mounts, and clamp mounts. Notch the table and the footrest to fit around the beam.

Assemble the parts that don't move or pivot with glue, screws, or nails. However, don't glue the table to the mounts — just bolt it in place. This will let you take the jig apart and store it. The beam must be left free to pivot between the mounts, and the knee rest should pivot on the knee rest mounts. The clamp assembly and the knee rest assembly must slide up and down the beam. Attach the jig to your workbench, running bolts through the cleats and the mounts.

(continued) ▷

BENCH-MOUNTED SHAVE HORSE — CONTINUED

1 **To use the jig, first adjust**
the clamp to the proper height.
Loosen the wing nut that holds it in
place. Slide it up or down the beam
until the rounded edge is about ⅛
inch above the surface of the workpiece you want to hold to the table.
Tighten the wing nut.

2 **If you wish to sit at a stool**
while you work, use the footrest to
operate the clamp. To clamp a workpiece on the table, push on the footrest. The beam will pivot, causing the
rounded edge of the clamp to push
down on the workpiece. To release the
clamp, lift your foot off the footrest.

3 **If you want to stand up and**
work, attach the knee rest to the
beam. Adjust the height and horizontal position of the rest so you can
press against it with your knee or
thigh — whichever is most comfortable for you. Press against the rest to
clamp the workpiece to the table; ease
up on it to release the workpiece.

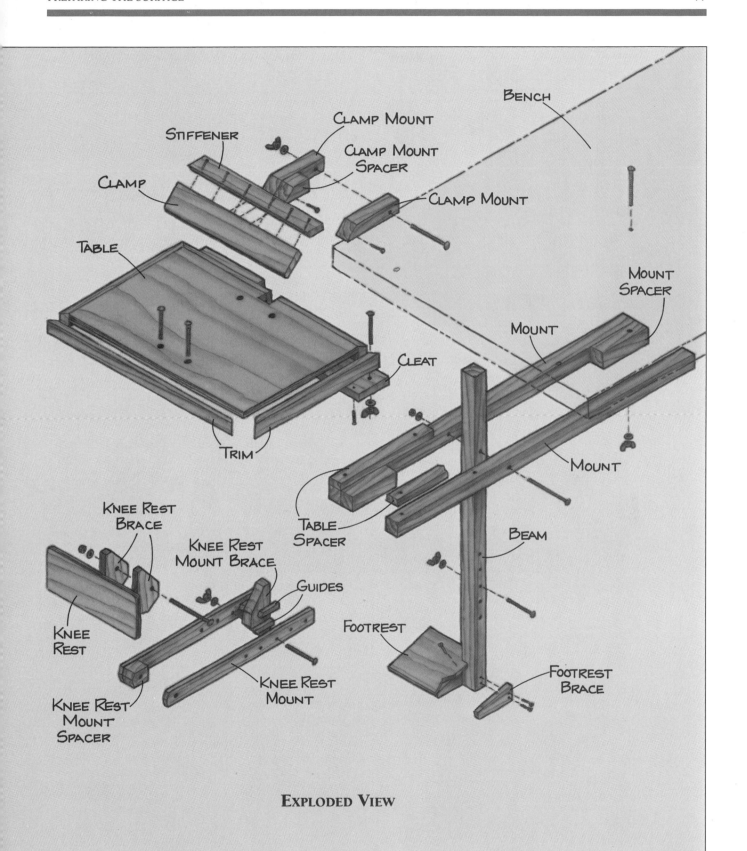

STIFFENER

CLAMP MOUNT

CLAMP MOUNT SPACER

BENCH

CLAMP

CLAMP MOUNT

TABLE

MOUNT SPACER

MOUNT

CLEAT

MOUNT

TRIM

TABLE SPACER

BEAM

KNEE REST BRACE

KNEE REST MOUNT BRACE

GUIDES

FOOTREST

KNEE REST

KNEE REST MOUNT

FOOTREST BRACE

KNEE REST MOUNT SPACER

EXPLODED VIEW

(continued) ▷

BENCH-MOUNTED SHAVE HORSE — CONTINUED

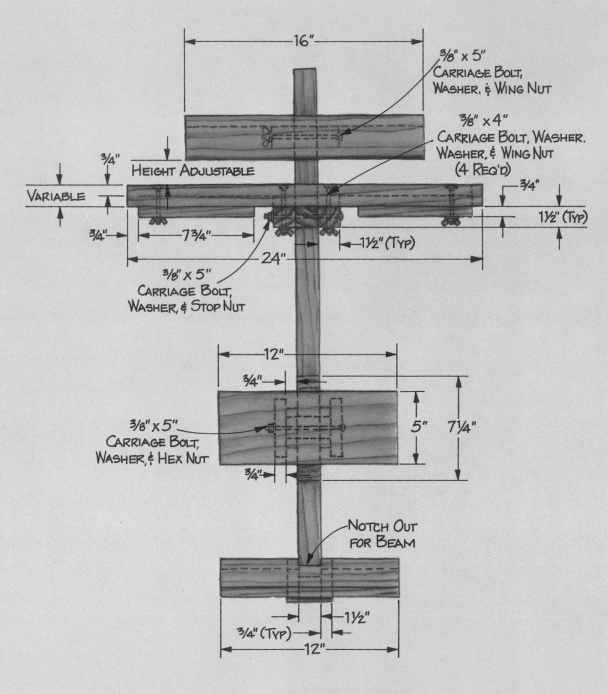

FRONT VIEW

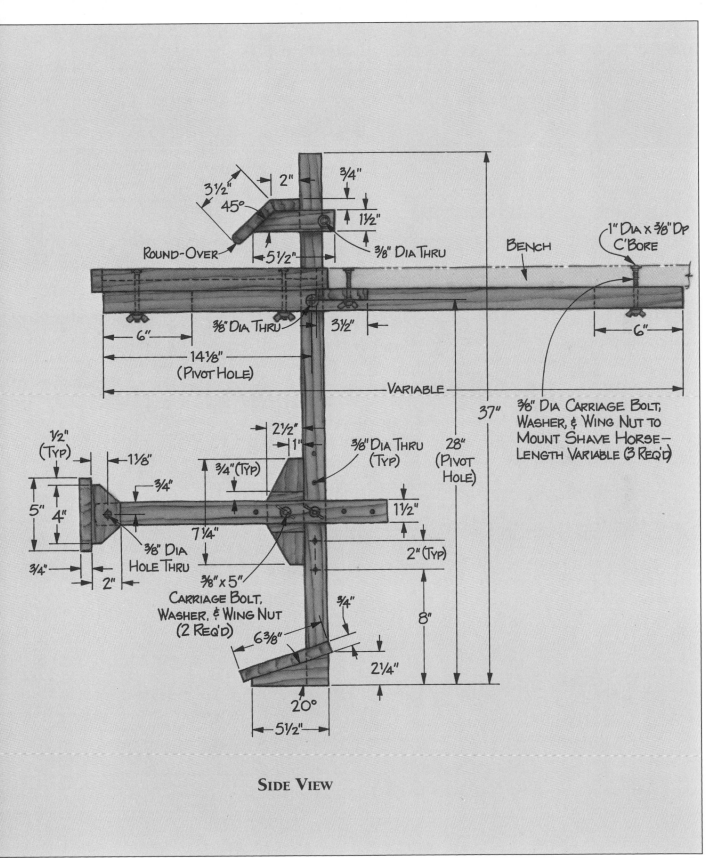

3½"

2"

45°

¾"

ROUND-OVER

5½"

1½"

⅜" DIA THRU

BENCH

1" DIA x ⅜" DP C'BORE

⅜" DIA THRU

3½"

6"

14⅛"
(PIVOT HOLE)

6"

VARIABLE

37"

⅜" DIA CARRIAGE BOLT, WASHER, & WING NUT TO MOUNT SHAVE HORSE— LENGTH VARIABLE (3 REQ'D)

½"
(TYP)

1⅛"

2½"

1"

¾" (TYP)

⅜" DIA THRU
(TYP)

28"
(PIVOT HOLE)

¾"

5"

4"

1½"

⅜" DIA
HOLE THRU

7¼"

2" (TYP)

¾"

2"

⅜" x 5"
CARRIAGE BOLT, WASHER, & WING NUT (2 REQ'D)

6⅜"

¾"

8"

2¼"

20°

5½"

SIDE VIEW

(continued) ▷

BENCH-MOUNTED SHAVE HORSE — CONTINUED

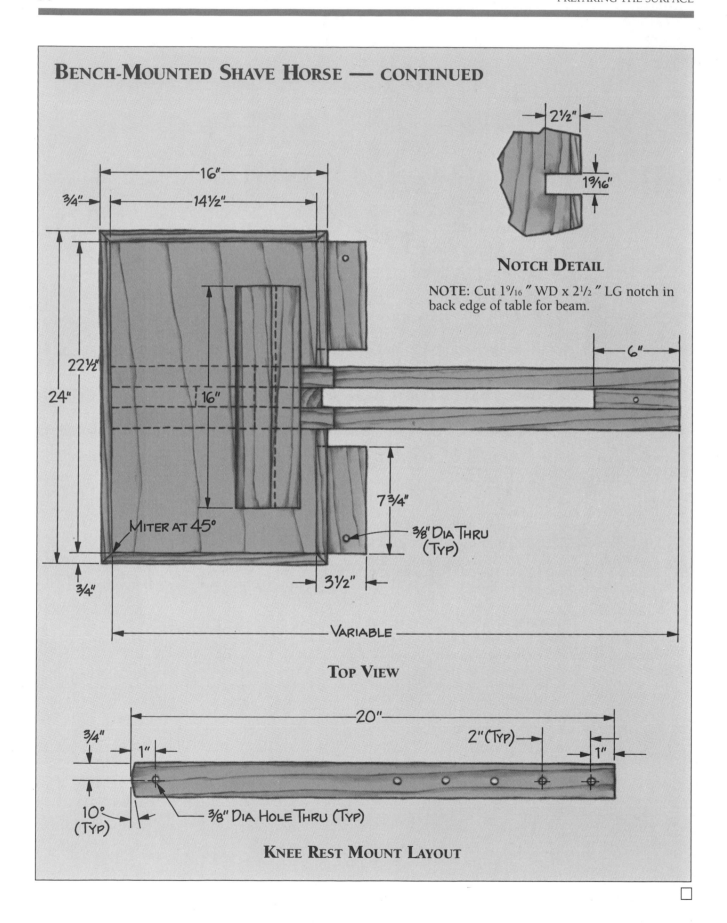

NOTCH DETAIL

NOTE: Cut 1⁹/₁₆″ WD x 2¹/₂″ LG notch in back edge of table for beam.

2½"

1⁹/₁₆"

16"

14½"

¾"

22½"

24"

16"

6"

Miter at 45°

7¾"

⅜" Dia Thru (Typ)

¾"

3½"

Variable

TOP VIEW

20"

¾"

1"

2" (Typ)

1"

10° (Typ)

⅜" Dia Hole Thru (Typ)

KNEE REST MOUNT LAYOUT

5

MODIFYING THE SURFACE

It may not be enough just to smooth and clean the wood surface. To achieve the degree of protection or the aesthetic effects that you want, you often have to *modify* some aspect of the surface before applying a finish.

The most common modification is changing the color of the wood. A stain or a dye adds visual interest to bland wood, artificially ages it, or causes it to look like another species entirely. Or you can alter the texture of the surface. Many building finishes will not form a smooth, continuous coat on some woods unless you level the pores and other natural irregularities with a wood filler or sealer. You can also adjust the way in which the wood absorbs a stain or finish. By judiciously applying sealers, you can prevent a stain from becoming too dark and even out the color from one surface of the board to another.

All of these modifications are accomplished by applying finishing chemicals to the wood. Although these materials are *not* finishes by themselves — they do not provide complete protection or enhancement — they often form the first tiers of a multi-layered chemical film. In this sense, they provide the *foundation* for the finish.

STAINING

Color is one of the most important components of good woodworking design; a change in color can profoundly alter the visual effect of a project on the viewer. Lighter wood tones seem more contemporary or casual, while darker tints are more traditional and formal.

When the natural wood tones don't convey the effect you want, you can stain the wood. There are several ways to do this. One of the easiest is to use a tinted finish — a "finish stain," as these materials are sometimes called. However, most experienced craftsmen prefer the traditional methods of staining or dying the wood. These allow you more control over the final color — you can easily adjust the shade as you mix and apply the stain. They also penetrate deeply into the wood. If the finish should be chipped or scratched, the damage isn't likely to show raw wood.

CHOOSING A STAIN

The many materials for changing the color of wood are usually grouped into these categories:

Chemical stains react either with the wood surface or with each other on the surface of the wood. In either case, the chemical reaction alters the wood color. Many of these stains are common household chemicals such as ammonia or lye; others, such as ferrous sulfate and nitric acid, are less familiar. (*SEE FIGURE 5-1.*)

Dyes are liquid coloring agents that penetrate the surface and bond to the wood fibers, much like cloth dyes hold fast to cloth fibers. The most common wood dyes are aniline dyes, intense colors derived from coal tars. (*SEE FIGURE 5-2.*) However, almost any colored solution can serve as a dye. For example, old-time craftsmen dyed wood with strong tea or the juice from walnut husks.

Pigment stains are opaque, colored powders, ground extremely fine and suspended in a vehicle such as linseed oil. (*SEE FIGURE 5-3.*) When applied to the wood, the oil dries and binds the pigment to the surface like paint. However, unlike paint, the layer of pigment is so thin as to appear semitransparent. Although the pigment obscures the grain slightly, the wood shows through.

Note: Many commercial stains contain both dyes *and* pigments; a few contain coloring chemicals as well.

Which of these staining materials should you choose? That depends on the wood you want to apply them to and the results you want to achieve. Each has advantages and disadvantages.

5-1 Many common chemicals will react with wood and change its color. Lye, for example, will darken most woods. Ammonia changes the color of cherry and oak. Steel wool soaked in vinegar produces a solution that creates a gray-brown color in woods that are high in tannic acid, such as oak and mahogany.

5-2 Aniline dyes come in powdered form, and must be mixed with the appropriate solvent — water, alcohol, or oil. They are highly concentrated; a little bit of powder will produce a large amount of liquid dye.

The advantages of chemical stains are that they penetrate very deeply and usually produce an even color. The chemical reaction takes place within the wood, and the substances that the chemical reacts with are distributed evenly throughout the wood, so the color change is uniform. And with a few exceptions, this change is permanent — it does not fade in time. The biggest disadvantage of chemical stains is that the range of colors is extremely limited. A given reaction produces just one color in a specific wood species, and often just one shade of that color. Also, chemical stains often involve hazardous chemicals and time-consuming methods of application. And since many chemical ingredients must be dissolved in water, these stains often raise the wood grain.

Dyes are much more versatile. There are many colors available, and you can mix these to produce an infinite variety of hues and shades. Aniline colors are rich, vibrant, and reasonably colorfast, although they will fade in time. (Some fade faster than others.) Depending on the vehicle, they can be made to penetrate just as deeply as chemical stains. Their chief drawback is that they are sometimes difficult to apply evenly. The best of the dyes are water soluble, and these raise the wood grain.

Pigment stains are available in the same variety of colors as dyes, are much easier to apply, and because they are usually oil-based, they do not raise the grain.

However, because the pigments are opaque, they will cloud the grain, making it appear fuzzy or unfocused. And they don't penetrate deeply — a shallow scratch will reveal raw wood. (*See Figure 5-4.*)

Experienced craftsmen generally prefer dyes for woods with strong grain, such as cherry, walnut, oak, ash, and mahogany. These hardwoods absorb the dyes evenly, and the intense colors enhance the grain patterns. Pigment stains will work well on all woods, although the results are not as spectacular as with dyes. Pigments are particularly useful for staining woods that might otherwise appear uneven or blotchy when dyed, such as pine and poplar. (*See Figure 5-5.*) They are also commonly used for woods with unimpressive, bland grain patterns, such as maple, birch, and basswood. Chemical stains, because they are so much trouble (and sometimes dangerous) to apply, are not much used. However, chemicals are worthwhile when you wish to reproduce an antique finish or artificially age the wood.

When choosing a stain, you must also give some thought to its vehicle and how it penetrates the wood. The deeper it penetrates, the richer and darker the color will appear. Water-based stains, because they are thin, penetrate deepest; oil-based stains penetrate least. Furthermore, the denser and more closed grain the wood, the more difficult it becomes for a stain to penetrate. (*See Figure 5-6.*)

5-3 The most common wood stains are pigment stains — finely ground colored powder suspended in a medium such as oil. When applied to the wood, the pigment collects in the scratch pattern left by the abrasive. As the medium cures, it binds the pigments to the wood surface.

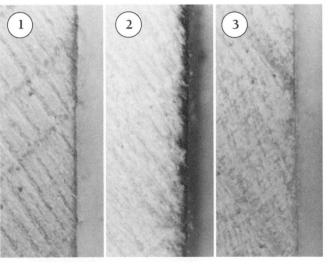

5-4 Both *chemical stains* (1) and water-soluble *aniline dyes* (2) penetrate deeply into the wood. This makes the colors richer and more permanent. *Pigment stains* (3) do not penetrate; they simply lie on the surface of the wood.

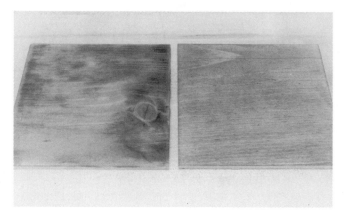

5-5 Some woods do not absorb
dyes evenly; these are best stained
with pigments. Shown are two pine
boards. The left board has been
stained with an aniline dye and
appears blotchy. The right one was
colored with a pigment stain. The
color is much more even.

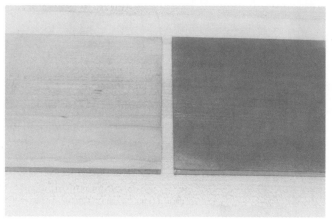

5-6 If you apply water-soluble
and oil-soluble dyes of exactly the
same color to a piece of rock maple,
the area with water-soluble dye will
appear much darker because water
is thinner and penetrates wood more
deeply than oil.

More vexing than choosing a type of stain is choosing a color. Several brands may use similar names — "Golden Oak," "Provincial," "Early American," and so on — but one manufacturer's version of a color can be noticeably different than another's. Furthermore, these colors vary depending on the type of wood to which they're applied. There may even be some variation within the same wood type. A sawyer's method of classifying wood is not as keen as a botanist's. For example, there are eleven major botanical species within the classification "red oak," and each of these reacts slightly differently to stains and other finishing chemicals.

If you are unsure as to what color you want, make a test strip on a scrap of wood that's left over from the project. Purchase small amounts of the colors that look best to you and apply them to the strip. Let the stains dry, then coat them with the clear finish you intend to use as a top coat. This will show you exactly what color each stain will produce on your project. (SEE FIGURE 5-7.)

If none of the ready-mixed colors produces the effect you want, mix two or more stain colors, or add dyes, artist's oil paints, or japan colors to alter a stain. Using a set of kitchen measuring spoons, carefully measure small quantities of the stains and/or coloring agents, keeping careful record of how much of each you add to the mixture. Then, when you arrive at the tone you want, you can mix up larger batches using the same proportions.

When trying to match a stain color — for example, staining a table to match a set of chairs — don't spend a great deal of time trying to get the colors precisely the same. Because wood tones are naturally variegated, the eye accepts (in fact, it expects) some variation. Instead, make sure the colors are within the same *tone range*. The basic hues must be approximately the same, but one color can be a shade lighter or darker than the other, and the eye will still accept them as matched.

APPLYING A CHEMICAL STAIN

Many chemical reactions are used to change the color of wood. To achieve them, the ingredients of each of these chemical stains must be mixed and applied in a specific manner. Here are a few of the most common stains.

A SAFETY REMINDER

Many chemical stains are dangerous and can irritate your skin, eyes, nasal passages, and lungs. Always wear rubber gloves and a full face shield when working with these materials. If the chemicals produce a vapor, as do nitric acid and ammonia, wear a respirator with either an acid vapor or ammonia cartridge, whichever is appropriate. In addition, stain the project outside or in a *ventilated spray booth*.

Nitric acid, when applied to most woods, speeds up the natural aging process. The surface grows much darker, developing an artificial patina. Purchase full-strength nitric acid from a chemical supply house, then mix a 14 percent solution by adding 1 part acid to 6 parts distilled water *in a glass container.* Using an old nylon bristle brush, paint the diluted acid on the surface of the project. Let it soak in for a few minutes, then warm the surface with a heat gun. The wood color will change almost instantly. (*See Figure 5-8.*) Continue warming the surface until all the acid is evaporated. Some craftsmen neutralize the acid by painting the surface with a mixture of 1 tablespoon baking soda to 1 pint of distilled water. This step prevents the acid from reacting with the finish, but is unnecessary as long as the acid is diluted to 20 percent or less and has evaporated completely before applying the finish. When the surface is completely dry, lightly sand the raised grain.

Household *lye,* or sodium hydroxide, will darken cherry, oak, and many other woods. To make a lye stain, dissolve 2 ounces of lye in 1 cup of distilled water in a glass container. In a separate container, stir 1 heaping tablespoon of cornstarch into 2 cups of distilled water. Add the cornstarch solution to the lye, stirring constantly. The resulting mixture should have the consistency of jelly. Using a nylon bristle brush, paint the lye paste on the project. Let the project sit 5 to 10 minutes, or until the wood stops turning color, then wipe off the paste with paper towels or an old rag. Neutralize the lye with a solution of 1 part distilled water and 1 part white vinegar, then rinse the surface with water — *lots* of water. Let the wood dry completely and lightly sand the raised grain. Dispose of extra lye paste by diluting it with water and flushing it down a drain.

A SAFETY REMINDER

When mixing acid and water, be careful to pour the acid slowly into the water, *not* the other way around. This will help protect you from a splash.

TRY THIS TRICK

Lye paste also makes an inexpensive paint and varnish remover. However, the surrounding air temperature must be 70° F or warmer.

5-7 A stain color often changes — sometimes dramatically — when a finish is applied over it. On this test strip, the left half is stained but *not* finished, while the right half is stained *and* finished. The two areas look very different. When preparing test strips for stains, you must also apply top coats to be able to judge the colors accurately.

5-8 As wood ages, it develops a dark *patina* — the wood cells near the surface become darker. To create an artificial patina, brush the wood with diluted nitric acid and warm it with a heat gun. As the temperature of the wood surface climbs, the surface will suddenly turn a dark brown.

Ammonia, like lye, will also darken cherry and oak — you can turn some woods almost black. During the late nineteenth and early twentieth centuries, craftsmen often "fumed" oak furniture by bathing it in ammonia vapor. Although household ammonia will work, aqueous ammonia (available from a chemical supply house) works much faster. (Aqueous ammonia is 28 percent pure ammonia, while household ammonia is usually less than 2 percent.) You can sponge the liquid ammonia on the wood, or use the "Portable Finishing Booth" on page 79 as a fuming chamber. (*SEE FIGURE 5-9.*) The advantage of fuming over sponging is that the fumes work faster, penetrate deeper, and don't raise the wood grain. If you apply the ammonia with a sponge, let the surface dry completely and lightly sand the raised grain before applying a finish.

Hydrated lime, or calcium oxide (available from any garden supplier or plant nursery), will darken (sometimes *blacken*) the color of oak, cherry, walnut, and mahogany, leaving white specks in the pores. When you stand back from the wood, the color looks gray or gray-brown. Like fumed oak, "limed" oak furniture was once stylish. To apply the lime to the wood, mix the powder with enough water to make a paste and paint it on the wood. Let the lime paste dry overnight, then wash it off with water. Let the surface dry completely and lightly sand the raised grain.

Ferrous sulfate will darken any wood with a high concentration of tannic acid, such as oak or mahogany. You can purchase ferrous sulfate from a chemical supply house, or make your own by soaking steel wool in a glass jar of cider vinegar for a week or so. Strain the rusty vinegar through a coffee filter, then paint it on the wood. For a darker color, apply several coats. Let the wood surface dry completely and sand the raised grain.

A SAFETY REMINDER

While the steel wool is soaking in the vinegar, leave the jar lid loose. The acid in the vinegar reacts with the metal to produce hydrogen gas. If you screw the lid on tight, the jar will explode.

Potassium permanganate (available from a chemical supply house) turns wood a purplish brown. The purple hue fades with time, but the brown remains. To apply the chemical, mix 1 ounce of potassium permanganate powder with 1 pint of distilled water. Brush the solution on the wood and let it dry completely. Lightly sand the raised grain.

5-9 To fume a project with ammonia, place it inside an enclosure such as the "Portable Finishing Booth". (See page 79.) Set up the enclosure *outside,* on a porch, or in an open shed, where escaping fumes will be blown away. If you use the booth, do *not* turn on the fan. Place the project inside the booth with a tempered glass bowl of ammonia on an electric hot plate. Set the hot plate to "warm" and seal the booth. Let the project bathe in the ammonia fumes until the wood is as dark as you want it. (You can continue fuming some woods until they turn almost black.) Depending on how long you leave the wood in the enclosure, you may have to add more ammonia from time to time.

APPLYING A DYE

Although craftsmen once extracted colors from plant materials such as tea and walnut husks, most dyes are now distilled from benzene or coal tar. These are commonly called aniline dyes.

Aniline dyes are available as water-, alcohol-, and oil-soluble. Most experienced craftsmen prefer water-based dyes. They penetrate deeply, are colorfast, and are least likely to interfere with whatever material you're using for a top coat. They work particularly well if you need to do additional sanding — because they penetrate so deeply, you're less likely to sand through the color and expose raw wood. Unfortunately, water-soluble dyes can be difficult to apply because they dry so fast. (*SEE FIGURE 5-10.*) In addition, they raise the wood grain.

Oil-soluble dyes do not raise the grain, and they dry more slowly, making them easier to apply. But they do not penetrate deeply and are not as colorfast. You can thin oil-soluble dyes with naphtha or lacquer thinner for better penetration; however, this also makes them dry faster. Alcohol-soluble dyes don't raise the grain, but they dry so quickly that they're almost impossible to apply evenly with a brush. They also dry too fast to penetrate deeply.

There are also *non–grain raising* stains, which are ready-mixed aniline dyes in a petroleum-based solvent. Although these dry almost as fast as alcohol-based dyes, you can mix them with a retarder to slow the drying time. This makes them easier to apply. However, the available colors of non–grain raising stains are limited, and you cannot adjust their shade as easily as you can with ordinary aniline dyes.

To apply an aniline dye, mix the color you want in a *glass container* — certain colors react with metal. If the color is not as deep or as dark as you'd like, add more dye to the solvent. For a lighter color, add more solvent.

If you're applying a water-based dye, raise the grain with water, let the surface dry completely, and lightly sand it before staining. The grain will raise again when you apply the stain, although not nearly as much as

5-10 When a stain dries faster than you can brush it on, you'll be able to see *lap marks* where each brush stroke overlaps the previous one. The resulting stain looks streaked and uneven. To prevent this, you must keep the stain wet as you apply it.

the first time. Some craftsmen prefer to wet the surface a second time and stain the wet wood — this keeps the dye from drying quickly, but it also limits penetration, and the color may appear lighter than intended.

When applying any of the three types, wipe or brush the dye on the wood. (SEE FIGURE 5-11.) Keep the surface as wet as possible without making the dye run, and try to overlap brush strokes as little as possible. If necessary, blend the stained areas with a rag soaked in the appropriate solvent to even out the color. This must be done *before* the dye dries. After the stain dries, sand lightly. Be careful not to expose raw wood.

Note: Dyes do not penetrate or bond well to the pores of open-grain woods such as oak or ash. For this reason, the large pores may appear lighter than the surrounding wood after staining. To compensate for this, you must apply a tinted wood filler after the dye.

TRY THIS TRICK

If the solvents are compatible, you can use aniline dyes to tint almost any finishing material — rubbing oils, shellacs, varnishes, waterborne resins, and pigment stains. However, the tints will fade in time. The dyes aren't as colorfast when suspended in a chemical film as they are when bonded to wood fibers.

APPLYING A PIGMENT STAIN

There are three types of pigment stains. *Oil-based stains* are pigments suspended in oil or a resin/solvent mixture, similar to thinned oil paint. *Water-based stains* are like thinned latex paint — pigments suspended in a resin/water mixture. *Gel stains* are pigments suspended in a pastelike chemical that changes from solid to liquid as you wipe it on the wood. (SEE FIGURE 5-12.)

All of these are extremely easy to apply. Of the three, gel stains are perhaps the easiest for several reasons. The gel keeps the pigment from settling to bottom of the can; you don't have to keep stirring the stain as you do with oil-based and water-based stains. The gel also keeps the stain from running, even on vertical surfaces. And because the vapor pressure of the gel medium is low, gels are less toxic than other stains. The drawback is that gels are harder to mix and much slower to apply than any other staining materials.

TRY THIS TRICK

You can make your own gel stains by purchasing white or clear thixotropic gels at a paint supply store, then tinting them with artist's oils or japan colors.

5-12 Gel stains are made with special *thixotropic* mediums. In an undisturbed state, these chemicals are about the same consistency as jelly. When you apply pressure to them by wiping them across the wood, they change from solid to liquid. Once the pressure is released, they solidify again.

5-11 One of the best applicators for dyes or pigment stains is an inexpensive foam rubber sponge brush. It holds more finish than ordinary brushes, but does not drip as easily.

To apply a pigment stain, simply brush or wipe it on, then wipe off the excess with a clean rag. If the surface is irregular or has a lot of cracks and crevices, wipe off the stain with a dry brush, then wipe off the brush on a rag.

Wiping evens out the stain color and controls the tone. (SEE FIGURE 5-13.) You can also adjust the tone by how you prepare the surface, as mentioned previously. As you sand the wood with progressively finer grits, the scratch pattern becomes smaller and shallower. The shallower the scratches, the less pigment that will collect in them, and the lighter the stain will appear. Finally, you can make the finish darker by applying several coats of stain. Let each coat dry before applying the next. But remember that with each coat, you cover the wood with an additional layer of opaque pigment. The wood grain will look cloudier after each application of stain. After the last coat, let the stain dry completely and sand lightly. Be careful not to expose raw wood.

STAINING TIPS

Here are a few techniques and formulas to help achieve better effects when staining:

■ End grain will absorb more stain than long grain, and will appear much darker. To even out the color, seal the end grain before applying a stain to the project. (SEE FIGURE 5-14.) You can make your own sealer by mixing 1 part commercially prepared (3- or 4-pound cut) white shellac to 4 parts denatured alcohol. Or mix 1 part aliphatic resin (yellow) glue to 5 parts water. Paint the sealer on the end grain surfaces with a fine brush, being careful not to coat the long grain.

■ Because of the way plywood veneer is cut from a log, plywood does not take a stain evenly. You can partially solve this problem by applying a special *plywood sealer* to the veneer before staining it.

■ To accent figured wood such as curly maple or bird's-eye maple, apply a thin coat of stain, let it dry completely, then sand lightly. (SEE FIGURE 5-15.)

■ You can make your own oil-based stains by mixing 1 part artist's oils to 1 part boiled linseed oil, then thinning the mixture to the desired consistency with turpentine. You can make water-based stains in a similar manner: Mix artist's acrylics and gel medium, then thin with water.

■ An oil-based stain, whether a dye or pigment, should not be used under a penetrating finish. Not only does it interfere with penetration, but the finish may partially dissolve the stain, causing it to bleed back out of the wood. When the finish dries, the color will look blotchy. To avoid these problems, use water-soluble dyes under penetrating finishes.

■ A finish that builds on the wood surface can also cause a stain to bleed. Or, if the two materials are incompatible, the stain may cloud the finish or keep it from curing properly. (This problem is common when applying lacquer over a stain, but it may occur

5-13 Wiping is the easiest way to control the tone of a pigment stain. The more you wipe, the more pigment you'll remove, and the lighter the stain will appear. For a darker stain, don't wipe as much.

5-14 You can even out the stain color by judiciously applying sealer to the surfaces that tend to absorb more stain. On the left board, the end grain absorbed more stain and appears much darker than the other surfaces. On the right board, the end grain was sealed before applying the stain. The color appears more uniform.

with other finishes as well.) To prevent this, segregate the stain and the finish by applying a *wash coat* of shellac — 1 part commercially prepared (3-to 4-

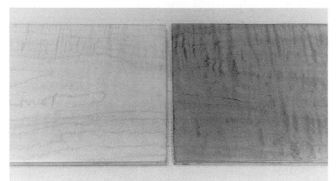

5-15 Figured wood shows both long grain and end grain on the same surface. When you apply a stain, it will penetrate more deeply into the end grain than the long grain. The two types of grain will appear as different shades of the same color. If you let the stain dry and sand the surface, you'll remove some color from the long grain, but not as much from the end grain. This will heighten the contrast between the two types of wood grain.

pound cut) white shellac mixed with 1 to 2 parts denatured alcohol.

■ In addition to staining the wood, you can also stain the finish after it's cured. Finish stains are commonly called *glazes*. Glazes artificially age the finish, giving it an antique look. (*SEE FIGURE 5-16.*)

5-16 Special stains called *glazes* are meant to be applied over cured finishes. They are thicker than ordinary stains, and are applied like pigmented stains — wipe them on, then wipe off the excess. The glaze darkens the finish and clings to the crevices, making the piece look old.

FILLING AND SEALING

Planing, scraping, and sanding will not always achieve as smooth a surface as you could wish for. Many species of wood have wide pores and other natural surface irregularities that cannot be smoothed over. These may be large enough to interfere with the smoothness and luster of the finish. They may also prevent the finish from forming a continuous coat, which may reduce the degree of protection afforded by the finish. When this is the case, you must *fill* the wood grain.

You may also want to *seal* the wood for a variety of reasons. Sealers, as the name implies, provide a barrier on the surface of the wood. This barrier prevents stains and other chemicals from penetrating the wood, and keeps whatever chemicals are already in the wood from bleeding out. If the stain or the natural oils in the wood are incompatible with the finish, you can oftentimes keep one from interfering with the other by separating them with a sealer. Sealers are also sanding aids — they will make the microscopic whiskers stand up. Then the hardened sealer holds the whiskers

upright so you can sand them off, which is why these products are often called sanding sealers. They sometimes serve as primers for the top coat. And they will fill small irregularities in the wood grain, although they will not smooth over large cavities as efficiently as wood fillers.

Fillers and sealers are applied after the wood has been sanded and, if you want to change the color of the wood surface, after the wood has been stained. Otherwise, the binders and resins in fillers and sealers will prevent stains from penetrating the wood. As mentioned previously, you can apply thinned sealers to end grain surfaces to prevent stains from penetrating too deeply, but this is the exception to the rule.

Note: Fillers and sealers are meant to be used as a foundation for finishes that build on the surface, such as shellacs, varnishes, lacquers, polyurethanes, and waterborne resins. They should *not* be used with penetrating finishes, such as drying oils and rubbing oils, since they will prevent these materials from soaking into the wood.

BLEACHING WOOD

While stains normally add color to wood or darken the tone, wood bleaches decolorize and lighten the wood. Unlike stains, which mask the true wood color, bleaches are highly reactive chemicals that attack the coloring agents or *extractives* in wood. They don't actually remove the color; instead, they break down the extractives, making them pale or transparent. They can also be used to break down unwanted wood stains.

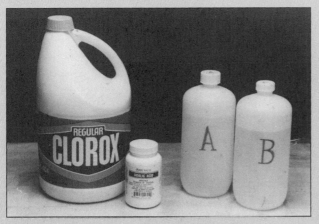

1 **Several common chemicals** can be used to bleach wood and wood stains. Chlorine (laundry bleach) will decolorize aniline dyes. Oxalic acid (available from chemical suppliers) will lighten the patina of old wood. However, the best all-around bleaches for both wood color and wood stains are two-part "A/B" solutions. Normally, "A" is a 25 percent sodium hydroxide (lye) solution, and "B" is a 35 percent hydrogen peroxide solution.

2 **Apply the sodium hydroxide** (A), let it soak into the wood, then apply the hydrogen peroxide (B). In some cases, you may get better results if you apply "B" immediately after "A," mixing them on the surface of the wood. The wood will begin to foam slightly. When the foaming stops, the wood will be lighter in color. Unless otherwise directed, there's no need to neutralize the bleach. Since the lye solution is alkali and the hydrogen peroxide is acid, the two liquids neutralize each other.

3 **If you want to lighten the** wood further, apply the solutions again. You can also apply a little chlorine bleach while the solutions are foaming to make them work faster. When the wood is as light as you want it, wash the surface thoroughly with water. Let it dry completely, then lightly sand the raised grain.

There are several ways to fill and seal a wood surface, and the best method normally depends on the type of wood grain. To fill and seal *open-grain* woods (woods in which the pores are large enough to see, such as oak, ash, walnut, rosewood, butternut, chestnut, and mahogany), apply a paste wood filler followed by a sealer. To fill and seal *closed-grain* woods (such as pine, poplar, basswood, and cedar), a heavy-bodied sealer with a high percentage of resins is usually sufficient. You can also use several coats of thinned finish. For woods with medium-size pores (such as cherry, maple, birch, and beech), you have your choice of methods — you can use a filler and a sealer, or several coats of sealer alone.

FILLING AND SEALING OPEN-GRAIN WOOD

To fill the pores of wood with an open or medium grain, first apply paste wood filler. The solids in the filler can be many different materials, but most experienced finishers prefer ground quartz, also called silica or *silex*. Quartz paste does not shrink as it dries, as some other materials do.

Fillers are available in several colors, and you can purchase untinted filler and color it with artist's oils or japan colors. If you want the wood grain to appear subdued, tint the filler so it's in the same hue range and *slightly* darker than the wood surface — there should not be much contrast between the two. To accent the wood grain, use a filler that's *very much*

darker than the wood. The contrast will make the pores stand out, but as long as the two colors are shades of the same hue, the wood will not look unnatural. (*SEE FIGURE 5-17.*)

TRY THIS TRICK

Make your own fillers by mixing very fine sawdust (from the same wood that you want to fill) with sealer or shellac to make a thin paste. This will shrink slightly as it dries, but it will be exactly the same hue and tone as the wood.

Thin the filler with the appropriate solvent to make it brushable. Brush a thick coat on the wood surface, let it dry to a dull sheen, then wipe off the excess with a piece of burlap, rubbing *across* the grain. (*SEE FIGURES 5-18 AND 5-19.*) The burlap will be too coarse to remove all the excess filler, so follow with a clean cloth, rubbing *with* the grain. Let the filler dry overnight, then *lightly* sand with the last grit used. Do not sand too much; you want to level the filler in the pores, but you don't want to expose any new pores.

After filling, it's a good idea to apply a sealer or a wash coat of thinned (1- to 1½-pound cut) shellac. There are several reasons for this. Fillers sometimes change the properties of the top coat — lacquers won't bond as well to the filled wood; polyurethane will lose some of its heat resistance. In addition, the filler may interfere with the way the finish cures. A sealer reduces these problems. Also, a sealer fills any minute imperfections that were not leveled by the filler, and it helps bind the filler in the pores.

5-17 You can achieve a variety of effects according to how you tint the wood filler. The oak board on the left was treated with a filler whose color matched the wood, while a much darker filler was applied to the right board. The darker filler emphasizes the grain pattern.

5-18 To apply a wood filler, thin it to the consistency of thick cream. Brush on a thin coat that completely covers the surface of the wood.

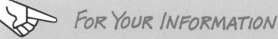

FOR YOUR INFORMATION

In addition to tinting the filler, you can also tint the sealer, if you wish. Tinted sealers are sometimes referred to as *undercoats*.

Brush the sealer on in a *thin* coat — if you put it on too thick, it may crack and weaken the top coat. Let the sealer dry completely, then sand with a slightly finer grit than last used. If you can, *wet* sand with silicon carbide paper, using water or mineral spirits as a lubricant — this will prevent the sealer from clogging the sandpaper. Clean the surface with a dry rag.

FILLING AND SEALING CLOSED-GRAIN WOOD

To fill and seal wood with medium-size or small pores, apply two or more coats of sanding sealer or wash coats of shellac. If the pores are extremely small, you can also use several coats of thinned finish. Many craftsmen prefer to use the finish as a filler because it ensures compatibility.

TRY THIS TRICK

Thinned shellac makes a good foundation for waterborne resins. If you use orange shellac, the natural amber tint will warm up the wood tones. When you apply the clear top coats, the finish will look more natural.

Apply at least two coats of the sealer, shellac, or thinned finish, brushing on each coat as thin as possible. Brush the first coat *against* the grain, let dry, then wet sand with a slightly finer grit than last used. (*SEE FIGURE 5-20.*) Brush the second coat *with* the grain, let dry, and wet sand with an even finer grit. (**Note:** There's no sense in sanding finer than 320-grit at this stage. If you've already reached that level, stick with 320-grit.)

Sand until the wood looks dull but the pores (which are filled with sealer) appear shiny. Be careful not to sand too much; you don't want to open up new pores. It's especially easy to sand away too much stock from the corners and arrises. To prevent this, use a sanding block and sand out from the center of a flat area in long strokes. When you've finished sanding, clean the surface with a dry rag.

Depending on the wood, it may take more than two coats to fill the irregularities. If you have to make more than three or four applications, however, you probably should have used a paste wood filler first.

SEALING ONLY

What if you simply want to seal the wood *without* filling the wood grain? There are times when you may want to knock off the whiskers or seal in the stain, but still preserve the natural texture of the wood. When this is the case, apply a single coat of sealer or wash coat of shellac and wet sand *very lightly* with a finer grit than last used.

5-19 Let the filler dry for 5 or 10 minutes, until the surface begins to glaze over and lose its shine. Using a piece of coarse burlap, wipe off the filler *across* the wood grain. Some craftsmen prefer to use horsehair (the material used to pad upholstered furniture) instead of burlap.

5-20 When sanding a sealer — or any finishing material — use silicon carbide wet/dry sandpaper, if you can. To prevent the paper from loading, lubricate it with a liquid that won't dissolve or otherwise affect the finishing material.

6

APPLYING THE FINISH

You may find the actual application of the finish to be an anticlimax after all the hard work required to arrive at this point. You've had to find your way through a labyrinth of possibilities to select the finish, then prepare and modify the wood surface to receive the chosen chemistry. Now, when you're finally ready to apply the finish, there are just four choices: You can wipe it on, pour it on, brush it on, or spray it on.

Furthermore, most of these application methods follow the same simple formula: Using whatever tool is called for, apply a coat of finish, let it dry, sand it smooth, and repeat as needed. There are a few tricks you should know to help ensure success, but all are fairly straightforward. If you've done everything right so far and use patience and care in applying the chemicals, this chore should progress smoothly.

In short, this is where you give your mind a rest and follow the directions on the can.

GENERAL FINISHING RULES

Although the method of application may differ from finish to finish, there are some general tips and techniques that apply to *all* finishes, no matter how they're applied.

■ *The finishing area should be at the proper temperature.* Finishes will not dry properly if the surrounding air temperature is too hot or too cold. For most finishes, the temperature should be between 70° F and 80° F.

■ *Cover the wood surface with a thin, uniform coat.* Spread the finish thin enough that it won't run or sag, but not so thin that it doesn't "flow out." The surface tension should level lap marks and brush marks as the finish flows into an even coat.

■ *Cover all wooden surfaces evenly,* inside *and* out, top *and* bottom. If you don't finish both faces of a wide board, the two surfaces will absorb and release moisture at different rates. This will cause the wood to cup or warp. This rule doesn't always apply. For example, it's traditional to leave the insides of drawers and cedar chests unfinished. But, in general, finish both sides.

■ While the finish dries, *protect it from dust* by erecting a "dust umbrella" over the wooden surfaces.

(*SEE FIGURE 6-1.*) You can also place the project in the "Portable Finishing Booth" shown on page 79.

■ *Remove any runs or sags before the finish dries completely.* If runs or sags develop in the partially cured surface, work them out with your fingertip and a little thinner. If you don't catch them until they dry completely, carefully shave them off with a razor blade.

■ *Sand the finish between coats.* This levels out any high spots in the coat, removes dust, and helps prepare the surface so the next coat makes a good bond.

■ *The more coats you apply, the more durable the finish becomes.* Thicker finishes also provide better protection.

■ When storing partially used containers of reactive finishes, *remove as much air as possible.* Remember that these products react with oxygen. (*SEE FIGURE 6-2.*) If the storage container is plastic, squeeze it until the finish level is near the top. If it's metal and there's a great deal of air in the top of the can, transfer the finish to a smaller container. You can also drop marbles into the can to reduce the amount of air.

■ Remember, *always follow the specific directions provided by the manufacturer.* The tips and techniques shown here are intended as *supplements*.

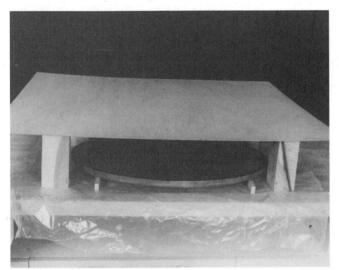

6-1 To keep dust from settling on a project as the finish hardens, make a "dust umbrella" from a scrap of plywood or particleboard. If the finishing area is dusty, it may also help to mist the floor and benchtops with water just before applying the finish. This will help prevent you from stirring up the dust as you work.

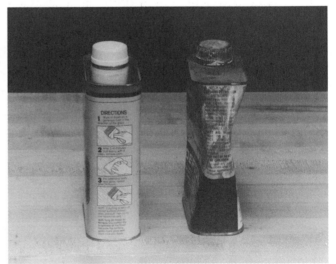

6-2 This can shows what can happen if there's too much air inside a container of a reactive finish. As this partially filled can of tung oil sat undisturbed for several months, it slowly reacted with the oxygen inside the can. In the process, the can collapsed and the finish turned into a gelatinous mess.

WIPING ON A FINISH

Wipe-on finishes require little time and effort —
you simply wipe them on, then wipe off the excess.
Because they are more diluted and slower to dry than
most finishing materials, you can apply an extremely
even coat with no lap marks. The drawback is that
each coat is very thin — sometimes only .0001 inch
thick. You must apply many more coats to achieve
the depth and degree of protection provided by
finishes that are applied in other ways.

Of the many wipe-on finishes, most fall into the
categories of drying oils (linseed oil, walnut oil, 100
percent tung oil) and rubbing oils (Danish oil, teak
oil, polymerized tung oil, tungseed oil). A few
thinned varnishes and polyurethanes are formulated
to be wiped on; although these are often touted as
"tung oil finishes," tung oil is rarely the major
ingredient.

FOR YOUR INFORMATION

Many craftsmen prefer wipe-on finishes with
tung oil or tung oil–derived resins in the formula.
Tung oil dries harder than other oils, has more
luster, is more water resistant, and doesn't yellow
as quickly. Ironically, 100 percent tung oil is not a
favorite — it's extremely slow to dry and often
looks spotty or uneven when cured. Straight tung
oil must be mixed with thinners and driers (making what is called tung*seed* oil) to render it easier
to apply.

WIPING TECHNIQUES

You can use a rag, sponge, brush, or even your hand
to apply a wipe-on finish. What you use to wipe the
finish on is not nearly as critical as what you use to
wipe it off. Use a clean, lint-free cloth to remove the
excess finish and spread it out in a thin, even coat.
(*SEE FIGURE 6-3.*)

Because wipe-on finishes are so thin, the first one
or two coats will penetrate the wood surface. The
deeper the finish penetrates, the better it bonds to the
wood. A deep finish also wears longer and provides
better protection — some wipe-on finishes can increase the hardness of the wood surface by 40 percent. For this reason, some craftsmen apply wipe-on
finishes with their hands, theorizing that body heat
will help the chemicals to penetrate. Tests have
shown this technique does not work; your hands

don't warm the finish more than a few degrees. However, heating the finish to between 100 and 120° F
prior to applying it will lower its viscosity, and this
does increase penetration. (*SEE FIGURE 6-4.*)

A SAFETY REMINDER

Do *not* warm combustible finishing materials
using an open flame and do *not* place the pan holding the chemicals directly on the burner. Use an
electric hot plate and a double boiler.

In addition to warming the finish, you may also
want to "sand in" the first coat with 320- or 400-grit
wet/dry silicon carbide paper. Sanding creates a slurry
of sawdust and finish that fills the pores and any other
minute irregularities or imperfections in the surface.
(*SEE FIGURE 6-5.*) It will also fill small gaps in the joinery.

After applying the first coat, wait several minutes to
let it soak in, then wipe off the excess. Be sure to get
all the unabsorbed liquid out from the corners and
crevices. The surface should have a shiny, wet look.

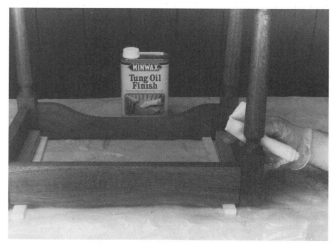

6-3 It's not important how you
apply a wipe-on finish, as long as
you saturate the wood surface. However, you should wipe it off with a
clean, absorbent rag. Fold or roll up
the rag as needed to get into crevices
and inside corners. Don't wipe away
too much finish; you should leave
the surface uniformly wet. Be sure to
discard the rag in a covered metal
container.

6-4 To increase the penetration of a wipe-on finish, heat it in a double boiler prior to application. Monitor the temperature with a candy thermometer, and don't let it get above 120° F. To avoid burning yourself, apply the finish with a ladle and spread it out with a brush. Wait for the finish to cool before wiping it off.

6-5 Although you can't use a paste wood filler underneath wipe-on finishes, you can achieve the same effect by sanding the first coat into the wood. This makes a slurry (or paste) of finish and sawdust which you can work into the pores. Wipe off the slurry *across* the wood grain, as you would a paste wood filler.

MIXING YOUR OWN WIPE-ON FINISHES

Although there are dozens of ready-mixed wipe-on finishes available commercially, some craftsmen prefer to make their own. The rationale is that a home-brewed wiping finish saves money and lets you adjust aesthetic and protective properties to suit yourself. The real reason is that it's a lot of fun to experiment. And if you follow the time-tested recipe for "wiping varnishes," it's hard to go wrong.

This traditional recipe calls for just three ingredients — an oil-soluble resin-bearing finish (such as varnish or polyurethane), a drying oil, and a compatible thinner. The classic wiping varnish mixture is

1 part varnish, 1 part boiled linseed oil, and 1 part turpentine. Another popular formula combines polyurethane, pure tung oil, and mineral spirits in equal amounts.

To create an original brew, study the chart below and pick one ingredient from each column. Blend them in equal amounts, or vary the ratio according to your own intuition. If you're undecided as to what ingredients and ratios might work best, make several different mixtures and compare them on test strips.

WIPING VARNISH INGREDIENTS		
Choose one from each column.		
RESIN	**DRYING OIL**	**THINNER**
Varnish*	Boiled Linseed Oil	Boiled Linseed Oil
Polyurethane†	Pure Tung Oil	Turpentine
Polymerized Tung Oil	Walnut Oil	Mineral Spirits

*Can be any kind — interior, tabletop, exterior (or "spar").
†Interior works best; exterior resins are too hard.

The penetrating coats may bleed back out of the wood for several hours. (This is especially a problem with open-grain woods.) If you don't wipe off the bleed-back, it will create shiny areas on the surface that make the finish look spotty and uneven. If necessary, continue wiping the surface every hour or so until the bleeding stops.

To build a film on top of the surface, apply additional coats of finish. One or more "building" coats over the penetrating coats is always a good idea; they make the finish more durable. Let each coat dry for a day (or more, if the manufacturer recommends it) before applying another. Sand between coats with wet/dry 400-grit paper, using the finish itself as a lubricant. Sand *very* lightly to prevent wearing through the thin coats. *Don't* sand after the last coat until the finish has cured completely. (See "Rubbing Out A Finish" on page 84.)

FOR YOUR INFORMATION

Because wipe-on finishes are usually so thin, they wear faster than other finishes. They should be reapplied when they grow dull or when the wood feels dry. This periodic maintenance is the price you pay for the ease of application.

POURING ON A FINISH

Catalyzing finishes, such as epoxies, are often poured on a surface. This allows you to build up a thick coat very quickly. You can also pour on certain reactive finishes, such as varnish and polyurethane, but they may need weeks to dry. It takes a long time for the oxygen in the air to permeate the thick coat and cure the finish completely. In catalyzing finishes, however, the catalyst or hardener is mixed evenly throughout the resin. No matter how thick the poured coat is, it usually sets in just a few hours.

POURING TECHNIQUES

Before pouring a finish, make sure the surface is perfectly clean and dry. Any oil, dirt, or dust on the surface may cloud the finish or prevent it from bonding to the wood. Moisture will condense inside the finish, fogging it. Also, make sure that the surface you want to pour the finish on is horizontal and *perfectly*

level. (SEE FIGURE 6-6.) **Note:** If you must apply epoxy or another catalyzing finish to vertical surfaces, brush it on.

A SAFETY REMINDER

Epoxies are highly dangerous chemicals. Wear a face shield, rubber gloves, and a respirator. If you are exposed to these finishes for more than a few hours at a stretch, or must work with them daily, cover any bare skin with Vaseline or "barrier cream." (See "Finishing Safety" on page 13.)

Combine the resin and the hardener in a disposable plastic container. Epoxies are very difficult to clean up, so it's best to use something you can throw away. Mix only as much finish as you can use before the epoxy begins to set. Check the container for this time.

Pour the mixture onto the surface, letting it flow out. (SEE FIGURE 6-7.) If you apply the finish to a flat surface with no lip, don't pour it deeper than approximately $1/16$ to $1/8$ inch, depending on the consistency of the mixture. Any more, and the finish will drip over the edges. If you wish to pour a deeper finish, you must make some sort of lip or enclosure.

If bubbles appear in the finish, use a hair dryer to blow a stream of warm air over the liquid before it sets. This will help the bubbles rise to the surface and dissipate. Some craftsmen may tell you to use your own breath — the carbon dioxide helps the bubbles to dissipate faster — but this is dangerous because you must remove the face shield and respirator and bring your face close to the toxic chemicals.

More than any other type of finish, it's important to let catalyzing finishes cure in a dust-free area. Rubbing out the dust dimples in the cured finish requires lots of elbow grease because epoxy becomes so hard. To save yourself a good deal of trouble, erect a dust umbrella (SEE FIGURE 6-1) or place the project in the "Portable Finishing Booth" shown on page 79.

If you wish to pour a finish on more than one surface of a project, let the finish harden on the first surface. Then turn the project and adjust it so the second surface is horizontal and level. Repeat until all the surfaces are covered.

Normally, pour-on finishes are applied to just one surface, and the others are coated with a compatible finish. For example, you may cover a bar top with epoxy, then apply polyurethane to the edges and bottom surfaces. Remember, you must finish *both* faces of tabletops and wide panels, or the wood will cup or warp.

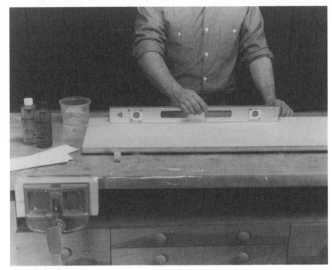

6-6 Before pouring an epoxy (or bar-top) finish on a surface, check that the surface is perfectly level. If not, shim up the low corners. If the surface is tilted at all, the finish will pool on the downhill side, and the depth won't look even.

6-7 Pour the finish on the surface. You can let it flow out by itself or use a piece of cardboard to spread the finish over the entire area. You can also tilt the board this way and that to help the finish spread out, but make sure you return the surface to a horizontal, level position before the finish starts to set.

BRUSHING ON A FINISH

The majority of finishes — shellacs, varnishes, polyurethanes, paints, brushing lacquers, and some waterborne resins — are meant to be brushed onto the wood surface. There are some special considerations for certain types of finishes, but generally the brushing techniques are similar from one finish to another.

BRUSHING TECHNIQUES

When preparing the finish, don't shake the can — this causes air bubbles. If the finish needs to be mixed, stir it gently. Don't apply the finish directly from the can. If there is dust or dirt on the surface of your project, the brush will pick it up and transfer it to the container, contaminating the finish. Instead, pour out the amount of finish you need into a separate container. If you haven't applied a sealer, dilute the first coat one-to-one with the appropriate thinner to make a primer. This will help the finish penetrate the wood surface and make a strong bond.

When loading the brush, dip about one-third of the bristles' length into the finish — don't load the brush all the way up to the ferrule. *(SEE FIGURE 6-8.)* When

6-8 Dip the brush less than halfway into the finish. If you load too much finish on the brush, it will flood the wood surface, creating runs and sags. If the brush does take on too much finish, don't wipe the brush on the side of the container; this loosens the bristles and may create bubbles. Instead, let the excess finish drip off the brush, or press the brush against the side of the container to squeeze the finish out of the bristles.

applying the finish, hold the brush as close to horizontal as you can. *(SEE FIGURE 6-9.)* You can apply thicker coats to horizontal surfaces than you can to vertical ones, but unless the horizontal area will see a great more wear and tear than the rest of the project, you should resist this temptation. Try to apply a thin, uniform coat to the entire project so the depth builds evenly.

TRY THIS TRICK

To get the finish uniformly thin, apply it with a partially loaded brush — sometimes called a "dry" brush. Dip the brush in the finish, wipe some of it off on a piece of scrap wood or cardboard, then apply the remaining finish to the project. This is also a great trick for preventing runs and sags, especially on complex surfaces.

If a bristle comes loose from the brush, pick it out of the finish before the film dries. You may want to keep a pair of tweezers handy for this eventuality. If

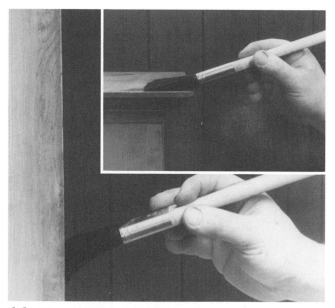

6-9 It's more important how you hold the brush in relationship to *gravity* than in relationship to the surface. Whether you are brushing a vertical or a horizontal surface, you want to hold the brush as horizontal as possible. This will prevent the finish from flowing too quickly out of the bristles and onto the surface.

you apply too much finish to an area, spread it out or remove it with the brush before it dries. As far as possible, brush with the grain. But don't brush too much. If the finish is slow drying, you'll work bubbles into the film. If it's fast drying, you'll leave lap marks and brush marks. *(SEE FIGURE 6-10.)*

Let the finish dry for the recommended time before applying another coat. Don't use a fan or warm air to speed drying. Not only do these methods stir up the dust, they may cause the finish to "skin over" — the molecules on the surface cure before those beneath them. On a vertical surface, this skin is likely to sag.

TRY THIS TRICK

To see if a finish has cured or hardened completely, test it with your thumbnail. If you can leave an indentation in the surface, it needs to dry longer.

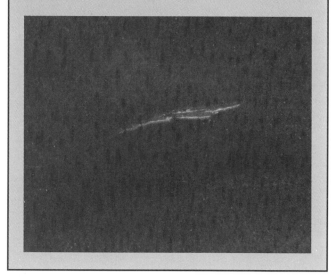

If the chemical film is hard when it dries (as varnish, polyurethane, and waterborne resins are), sand between coats with 250- to 320-grit sandpaper. If it's soft (as lacquer and shellac are), use 400-grit sandpaper — the finer grit will help keep you from sanding through the soft film. *(SEE FIGURE 6-11.)* If the paper loads quickly, stop sanding — the finish probably hasn't hardened sufficiently.

If you're applying a solvent-releasing finish (such as lacquer or shellac) that partially dissolves preceding coats, you don't absolutely need to sand between coats. Some craftsmen prefer to sand every second or third coat to allow the film depth to build faster. However, don't wait too long. The more coats you apply before sanding, the more uneven the surface becomes.

After sanding, wipe the surface clean and dry. Apply successive coats with the same techniques. However, don't sand after the last coat until the finish has cured completely. (See "Rubbing Out a Finish" on page 84.)

6-10 Don't brush too much, especially if the finish dries fast. If the finish dries as you brush, you'll leave lap marks. These greatly increase the time you must spend sanding between coats.

6-11 Use silicon carbide wet/dry paper to sand between coats. For reactive finishes, lubricate the paper with mineral spirits. For solvent-releasing and coalescent finishes, use water. Lubricant helps to float away tiny particles of abraded finish, and keeps them from clogging the sandpaper.

SPECIAL BRUSHING CONCERNS

Depending on the type of finish you apply, there may be special considerations or brushing methods:

Shellac — When stored in a liquid state, shellac degrades with time. For this reason, many craftsmen prefer to mix their own, making a fresh batch for each project. When mixing shellac, use 95 percent denatured *ethyl* alcohol — too much methyl alcohol (wood alcohol) can reduce the quality of the finish.

Pay particular attention to the *cut* — the ratio of shellac solids to alcohol. One pound of shellac flakes dissolved in 1 gallon (8 pounds) of alcohol is referred to as a 1-pound cut. You may prefer to think in smaller quantities, since most home craftsmen rarely have use for an entire gallon of finish. One ounce of flakes in 1 cup (8 ounces) of alcohol makes a 1-pound cut; 2 ounces to a cup makes a 2-pound cut; and so on. Most craftsmen prefer 1- or 2-pound cuts for wash coats and primers, and 2- or 3-pound cuts for successive coats. Because cuts with higher amounts of solids won't flow out properly, they look uneven and require more sanding.

 WHERE TO FIND IT

You can purchase shellac flakes and ethanol from Garrett Wade (see page 23), Lee Valley (see page 24), or the Wood Finishing Supply Company (see page 24).

Varnishes — Of all the brush-on finishes, varnishes are the slowest to dry. Depending on the temperature and the humidity, you may have to wait 48 hours or more between coats. This has some advantages. You can "work" a varnish finish with a brush for a much longer time than other finishes, getting each coat as even and as level as possible. Many finishers brush varnish on with the grain, then brush it across the grain, and finally use just the soft tip of the brush to gently wipe the liquid film smooth with the grain again. (This is sometimes referred to as "tipping.")

The slow drying time also gives you a longer working window to remove runs and sags.

Polyurethane — In comparison to other brush-on finishes, polyurethane has a medium drying time. It also has a sensitive time "window" inside of which you must apply the next coat. For most polyurethanes, this is 8 to 12 hours. (However, check the directions on the can — sometimes the window lasts as long as 2 days.) If you don't wait long enough between coats, the finish will not be hard enough. You won't be able to sand the surface, and the fresh coat may dissolve the preceding one. But if you wait too long, the finish will become too hard for another coat to bond to it. Once the window has passed, you must "scuff sand" the cured finish with 220-grit paper to give a new coat a rough surface to hold on to.

Brushing lacquers — Because brushing lacquers are essentially spraying lacquers with retarders added to slow the drying time, many of the same precautions apply for both finishes. Refer to "Spraying On a Finish" on page 75 for instructions on how to mix lacquer with retarders or flow-out solutions to prevent blushing, orange peel, and other problems. Also, wear a respirator to protect yourself from the highly volatile solvents, even in a well-ventilated area.

Although you can sometimes apply other finishes over lacquer, don't apply lacquer over them — lacquer solvents dissolve many reactive and coalescing films. This also applies to most stains and fillers. You may have to use special lacquer-compatible stains and fillers or seal the surface with a wash coat of shellac.

Brushing lacquers are tricky to apply evenly. For this reason, most experienced finishers reserve them for small projects, applying them in superthin coats.

Waterborne resins — Brush-on waterborne resins are also difficult to apply, perhaps more difficult than any other brush-on finish. However, because of the intense research now being done on low-VOC finishes, there are new and better formulas almost every month. In the near future, they may become easier to apply than shellac or polyurethane.

When applying waterborne resins, use a nylon bristle brush; natural bristles and certain other synthetics absorb water and swell up. Dampen the bristles with distilled water *before* you start to help load the finish on the clean brush.

If you need to thin waterborne resins, use distilled water. The impurities in hard water can precipitate "gel specks" in the finish. If the finish dries too fast, add a small amount (1 ounce per gallon) of propylene glycol as a retarder. If it foams or bubbles as you brush it, add half-and-half cream a few drops at a time until the foaming stops. Don't add any more cream than 1 ounce per gallon.

Store waterborne resins at room temperature; don't let them freeze. (*SEE FIGURE 6-12.*) When disposing of excess finish, don't think that just because it cleans up with water you can flush it down a drain. Hard water turns waterborne resins into a sticky glop that clogs the plumbing. Dispose of the excess as you would any other finish. (See "Finishing Safety" on page 13.)

6-12 If waterborne resins freeze, they will be ruined. The wood shown was coated with a water-based varnish that was stored in a garage and froze during a cold snap. The finish won't dry properly; it just sits on the wood and looks ugly.

CHOOSING AND CARING FOR A BRUSH

Several cults have grown up around one type of brush or the other. Currently, the Chinese hog bristle brush has attracted the most zealots, and true believers even swear that hogs raised in northeast China produce the best bristle. However, there are also those who profess their faith in badger bristle, ox hair, even the lowly, disposable foam rubber brush. But mythology aside, most objective woodworkers who have experience with several types of brushes report that any high-quality brush — natural or synthetic — will work well for most finishes.

1 **What determines a quality** brush? The most important part, of course, is the bristles. These should be slender, slightly tapered, with the wide end at the ferrule, and split or "flagged" at the tip. The flags help to control the flow of finish and diminish brush marks. The bristles should also be springy, but not so stiff that they won't bend easily. Finally, they should be about half again as long as the brush is wide. A 2-inch-wide brush, for example, should have 3-inch-long bristles.

2 **The ferrule — the metal ring** around the bristles — should hold the bristles securely to the handle. To test this, strike a new, unused brush against your hand. A few bristles may work loose at first — this is normal — but not after a moment or two. The handle should also feel comfortable in your hand.

3 **Inexpensive, disposable foam** brushes serve well for some finishes, particularly varnish, polyurethane, and waterborne acrylics. They hold a lot of finish and don't leave brush marks. But it's easier to regulate the flow of finish with a bristle brush. Also, the solvents in shellac and lacquer will dissolve the foam.

(continued) ▷

CHOOSING AND CARING FOR A BRUSH — CONTINUED

4 If you choose a natural-bristle brush, remember that it requires a short break-in period. Some craftsmen suspend new brushes so the bristles soak in mineral spirits or turpentine for a day or two. They then wipe the brushes on scrap wood for a few minutes, and clean them with soap and water.

5 Always clean a bristle brush immediately after using it. Wipe off the excess finish on a scrap of wood or cardboard. Swirl the bristles in solvent and work them against the side of the can. Groom the bristles with a "brush comb," and swirl them in clean solvent. Finally, wash with soap and water.

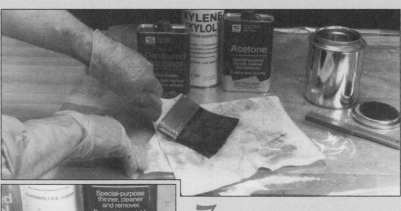

6 Store the brushes by hanging them with their bristles down — never rest a brush on its bristles. Some craftsmen wrap them in paper to keep the bristles from becoming contaminated with dust. Don't use plastic for this purpose; it prevents the bristles from drying. You want the bristles to dry completely before using the brush again, or they will lose their spring.

7 If you allow finish to harden on a brush, don't throw it away! You can save it by soaking it in paint remover. Or, make a super brush cleaner by mixing 2 parts toluol or xylol, 1 part acetone, and 1 part denatured alcohol. Let the brush soak in the cleaner overnight, and comb the hardened finish out of the bristles. Rinse the brush in fresh cleaner, then wash it with soap and water.

SPRAYING ON A FINISH

Two types of finish are best applied by spraying — lacquers and waterborne resins. However, you can spray almost any finishing chemical, provided you have the proper equipment and mix the material to the proper consistency. The advantage of spraying is that it's very quick, and once you acquire the knack, the finish goes on very evenly with no brush marks or lap marks. This reduces the time required to sand the finish between coats. The trade-off is that spraying requires expensive equipment, lots of room, and a good deal of practice.

SPRAY EQUIPMENT

In a pinch, you can spray very small projects with a hand-pumped atomizer or a spray bottle. However, for anything bigger than your fist, you need a *sprayer* and *spray gun*. There are two types available — high-volume, low-pressure (HVLP) systems; and low-volume, high-pressure (LVHP) systems.

An LVHP sprayer is driven by an air compressor, which pumps air into a metal tank where it is stored under high pressure. A small amount of air is bled through the spray gun. The air blows over a siphon, draws a steady stream of finish from a reservoir, then blows the finish out a nozzle, vaporizing it in the process.

An HVLP system normally uses a turbine instead of a compressor to maintain a steady air flow. There is no holding tank, so the pressure never builds very high. Instead, the air is blown directly into the gun, where it forces the finish through a small tube and out the nozzle. Although the guns on both systems look similar and produce the same result, they work very differently. You cannot use an LVHP gun on an HVLP system. *(SEE FIGURE 6-13.)*

LVHP systems are very versatile; you can hook sanders, polishers, and many other air-powered tools to the air compressor. On the other hand, if the only tool you want to use with your system is the spray gun, an HVLP turbine offers distinct advantages. It's lightweight, much easier to set up, and has a very high *transfer efficiency* — about two-thirds of the finishing materials end up on the wood surface, versus one-quarter with an LVHP system. Because of this, there's much less "overspray" — finish that ends up on the floor, on the walls, or in the air.

To contain overspray, you also need a *spray booth* — a ventilated room or enclosure. *(SEE FIGURE 6-14.)* This applies whether you spray lacquers or waterborne resins. There is a misconception among some craftsmen that you don't need a spray booth to apply waterborne resins because they contain so few organic solvents. Unfortunately, *all* finishing materials produce dangerous vapors that must be evacuated, especially if you're using an LVHP spray system. Unlike lacquers, however, waterborne resins don't require you to have *explosion-proof wiring* in the spraying area. (See "Finishing Safety" on page 13.)

6-13 *Low-volume, high-pressure spray systems* (left) use an air compressor and a holding tank to provide a steady stream of air. *High-volume, low-pressure systems* (right) usually employ a turbine. Although turbine systems are slightly more expensive than air compressor systems, they cost less to operate. They deposit more finish on the project with less overspray, so you save money on materials.

SPRAYING TECHNIQUES

Spraying is an operation that requires some expertise. If you've never done it before, you should practice on scrap wood or old pieces of furniture until you develop the knack *before* you spray a good project.

The most important technique when spraying is *planning* — think about how you're going to approach the surfaces of a project, and in what order, *before* you pull the trigger on the spray gun. Many experienced finishers recommend dry runs — go through the motions of spraying a project with an unloaded spray gun before you actually apply the finish.

Thin the finishing material to the proper consistency. This will vary for the material and the type of spray system; generally, spray mixtures are much more watery than any other finishes. Depending on the temperature and the humidity, you may also have to add retarders or flow-out agents. If it's warm, the finish may dry too fast and develop a bumpy texture called "orange peel." To correct this, replace some of the thinner with retarder when mixing the finish. Retarder will also help on humid days when the finish "blushes" — develops milky spots. If the surface is contaminated, the finish may not flow evenly, resulting in dimples or "fish-eyes." A flow-out agent (sometimes called a "fish-eye eliminator") may correct

this if the contamination isn't too bad. Flow-out additives can also help with orange peel.

Adjust the nozzle to get a good spray pattern — most finishers prefer a wide oval. (*SEE FIGURE 6-15.*) Also adjust the air flow and/or pressure. The air should blow through the gun with enough force to atomize the finish; otherwise, the gun will sputter and spit. But if the pressure or the air flow is too high, the finish will hit the wood and bounce back.

As you spray, keep the nozzle of the gun a constant distance from the project — 6 to 12 inches, depending on the spray pattern and the finish. Resist the temptation to swing your arm in an arc; this will deposit an uneven finish on the wood. Move the nozzle from side to side or up and down in a straight line, lapping each pass. (*SEE FIGURE 6-16.*)

Start spraying with the nozzle pointing off to the side. Don't pull the trigger when the gun is aimed directly at the project — for an even finish, the gun should be moving when it's depositing the material on the project. Spray horizontal surfaces from side to side, working away from you. Spray vertical surfaces from the top down. (*SEE FIGURE 6-17.*) Coat the edges, turnings, and other small surfaces first, then spray the wide, flat areas.

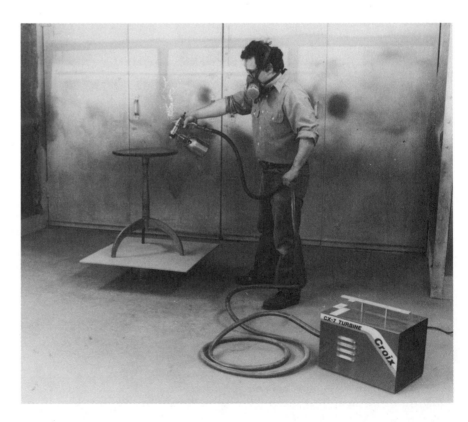

6-14 To spray finishes safely, you must have a ventilated spray booth to evacuate the overspray and fumes. If you're spraying lacquer or other finishes with flammable solvents, this booth must be equipped with explosion-proof wiring.

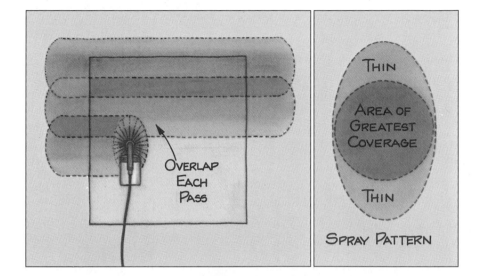

6-15 Adjust the nozzle to get a wide, oval-shaped spray pattern. This pattern deposits more finish in the middle of the oval than toward the ends. To compensate for this, overlap each pass about one-third the width of the oval.

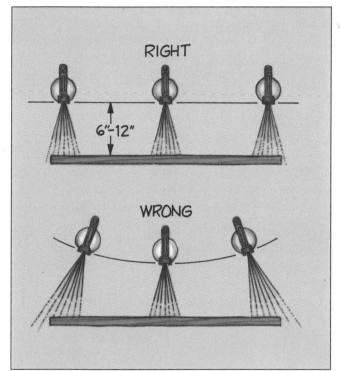

6-16 When spraying, move your arm from side to side in a straight line. This keeps the nozzle the same distance from the project, so the spray pattern remains the same size and the finish is deposited evenly. Don't swing your arm in an arc; the finish coat will be too thin at the start and end of the arc, and too thick in the middle. Where it's thin, the coat may suffer from orange peel. Where it's thick, it may run or sag.

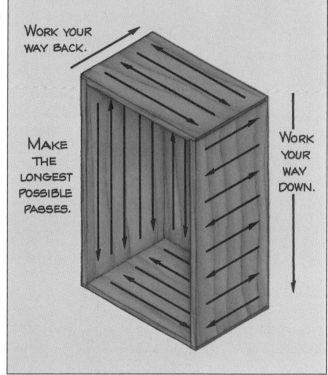

6-17 Most finishers prefer to start spraying a project at the top. Spray horizontal surfaces by coating the closest areas first, and then work away from you. Spray vertical surfaces by starting at the top and working down. You'll find it's easiest to move your arm from side to side when spraying large, broad *outside* surfaces. For *inside* surfaces and small areas, move your arm in the direction that allows the longest pass.

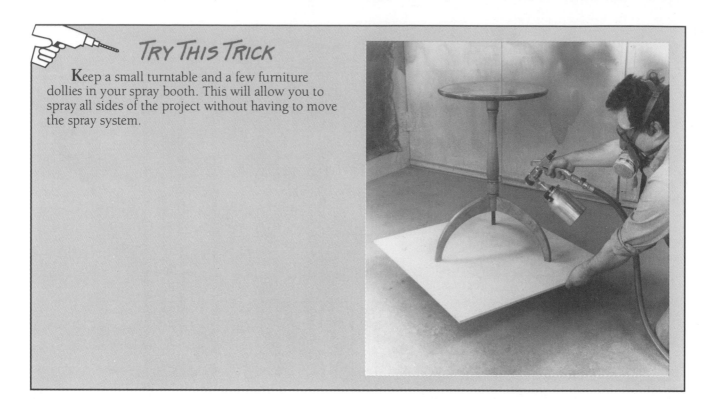

TRY THIS TRICK

Keep a small turntable and a few furniture dollies in your spray booth. This will allow you to spray all sides of the project without having to move the spray system.

As you spray, maintain a thin, wet, even coat. If the coat is too thin, it won't flow out properly and may develop orange peel. If it's too thick, it will run or sag. Only experience will help you to apply exactly the right amount of finish to the surface.

If the finish requires it, spray on a sealer or a primer first, then begin to build up additional coats. Let each coat dry the recommended time before sanding. If you're spraying lacquer, sand with 400-grit wet/dry paper to avoid cutting through the soft chemical film. Waterborne resins dry harder, so you can use coarser 320-grit paper. After each coat, clean the spray gun thoroughly.

SPECIAL SPRAYING CONCERNS

Although the general spraying techniques are similar, there are several special considerations and precautions for applying lacquers and waterborne resins.

Lacquers — Always wear eye protection and a respirator with an organic-vapors cartridge to protect yourself from the solvents. Change the cartridge the *minute* you begin to smell the fumes — this tells you that the cartridge is starting to wear out. If you're using an LVHP system, you should also wear a long-sleeve shirt, long pants, and a hat.

Spray lacquers contain only 10 to 15 percent solids. Because of this, you may have to apply many more coats than you would with other finishes to build sufficient depth. However, you can save time when sanding — lacquer is much easier to sand than most other materials. And because a fresh coat of lacquer partially dissolves the coat beneath it, you don't have to sand after each coat. If you wish, you can sand every second or third application.

Waterborne resins — You should take all the precautions when spraying waterborne resins that you do when spraying lacquer. However, because of the low organic solvent content, you'll find your respirator cartridges last a great deal longer.

Always use stainless steel equipment; water will corrode ordinary spray guns. Also use a slightly smaller orifice and needle than you would for spray lacquers. As you set up, make sure the air filter and water trap on the system are perfectly clean — any stray oil or contaminated water may ruin the finish. For the same reason, be careful how you thin the finish — use either distilled water or a special water-based reducer, as recommended.

When spraying, don't let the gun sit more than 10 or 15 minutes without pulling the trigger. Waterborne resins will dry and clog the nozzle much faster than lacquer. And unlike lacquer, waterborne resins don't dissolve themselves and the gun won't clean itself as you spray. When spraying a large project, you may have to stop and clean the gun now and again.

PORTABLE FINISHING BOOTH

One of the most persistent problems when finishing a project is *dust*. As dust particles settle onto freshly finished surfaces, they become imbedded in the chemical film, ruining the smoothness and luster of the finish. It's ironic that woodworking shops are among the dustiest places on earth.

There are several ways to deal with this problem, but perhaps the most effective is to create an *enclosed* dust-free area especially for finishing. This doesn't have to be a separate room or a permanent booth — few of us have the space to spare for a dedicated finishing room. Instead, make a *portable* knock-down finishing booth that rests on the workbench. This is a tentlike enclosure, large enough to hold small and medium-size projects. When in use, it blows clean, filtered air into the plastic tent and keeps dust from settling on whatever is inside. **Warning:** This booth can *not* be used as a spray booth; it does *not* evacuate the harmful vapors from the finishing area.

1 When not using the booth, fold it up flat, as shown. As long as the fan isn't large, the entire jig should be light enough to carry easily. This makes it convenient to store and set up.

2 To set up the booth, first clean up your workbench and wipe it with a tack cloth to remove any dust. Place the booth on the bench and unfold the top and sides. Place the project to be finished inside the enclosure. With the front flap rolled up and out of the way, apply the finishing materials.

(continued) ▷

PORTABLE FINISHING BOOTH — CONTINUED

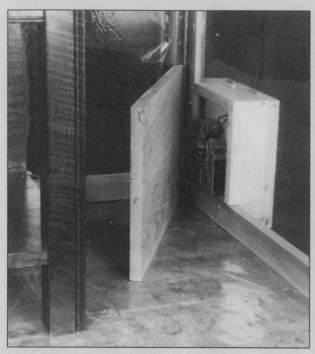

3 **Allowing the fan to blow** directly on the project may cause the finish to skin over and sag. To prevent this, use a scrap of wood as a baffle, redirecting the air stream away from the project surface.

4 **Roll down the front flap and** secure it to the front edges of the sides with the Velcro strips. Check that the filter is clean, then turn on the fan. Because the fan creates a positive pressure with filtered air inside the enclosure, no dust will seep in the cracks. You can continue working inside the shop — even saw and sand wood — without worrying about ruining the finish. Check the filter from time to time and clean it as necessary.

To make the portable finishing booth, build four wooden frames for the top, back, and two sides. These frames will form an enclosure that should be no wider or deeper than your workbench. Attach the frames to each other with piano hinges so the two sides fold toward each other and the top folds over the sides.

Purchase a small fan, just large enough to create a *gentle* air flow. You don't want a tornado inside the enclosure! Build a small box for the fan and attach the exhaust end to one side frame, near the

bottom rail. Fashion a filter for the intake end from cheesecloth or furnace filter material. Wire the fan motor through a rheostat to adjust the speed.

Cover the frames with a durable plastic film, stapling the plastic to the rails and stiles. Also attach a flap of plastic to cover the front. Attach self-adhering Velcro strips to the inside edges of the plastic flap and the front edges of the sides. These will allow you to close the flap securely. The enclosure doesn't have to be airtight, but all openings should be as small as possible.

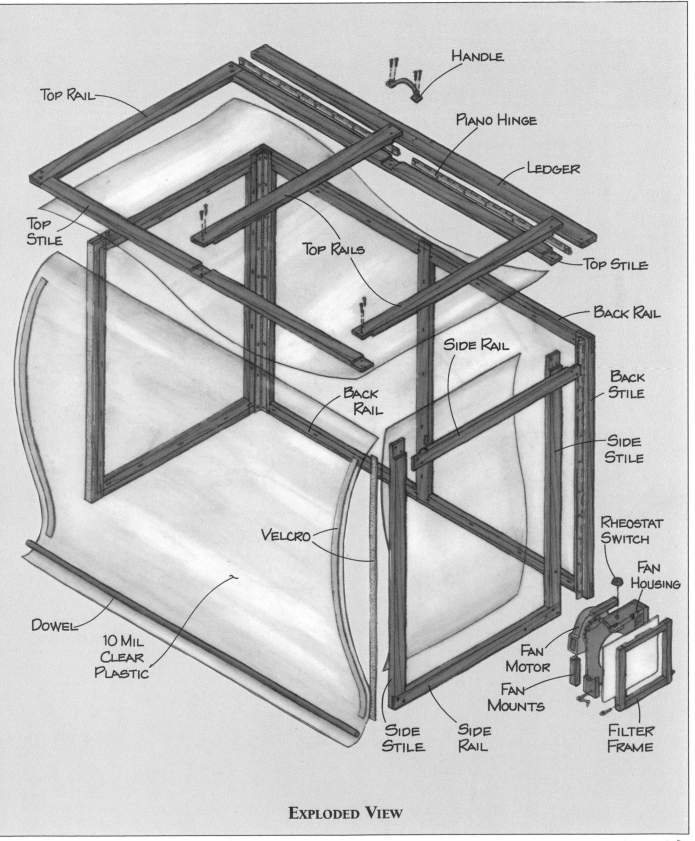

HANDLE

PIANO HINGE

LEDGER

TOP RAIL

TOP STILE

TOP RAILS

TOP STILE

BACK RAIL

SIDE RAIL

BACK STILE

BACK RAIL

SIDE STILE

VELCRO

RHEOSTAT SWITCH

FAN HOUSING

DOWEL

10 MIL CLEAR PLASTIC

FAN MOTOR

FAN MOUNTS

SIDE STILE

SIDE RAIL

FILTER FRAME

EXPLODED VIEW

(continued) ▷

PORTABLE FINISHING BOOTH — CONTINUED

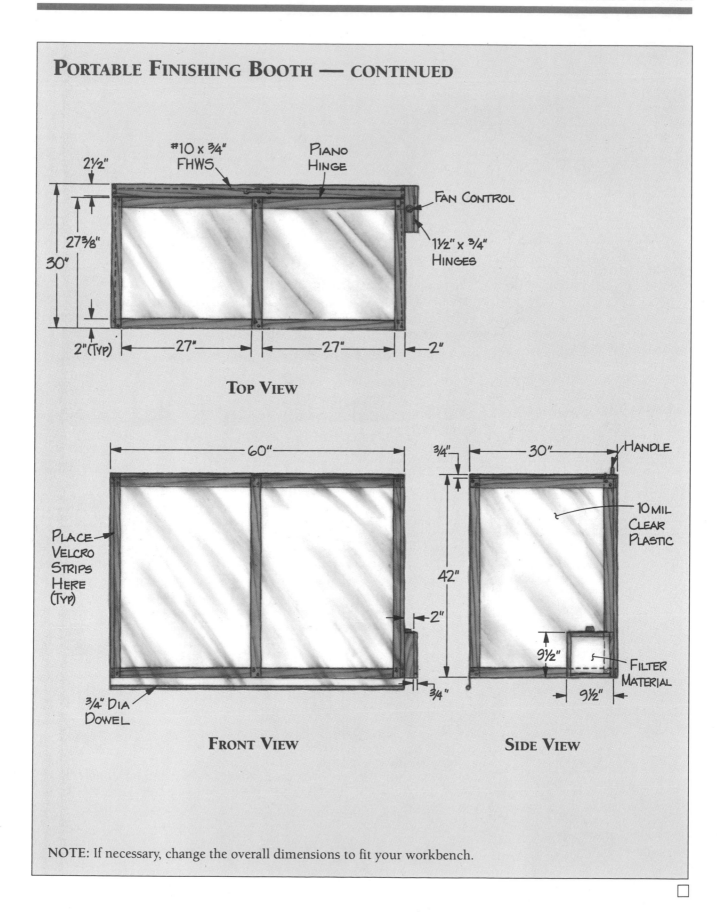

#10 x ¾" FHWS

PIANO HINGE

FAN CONTROL

1½" x ¾" HINGES

2½"

27⅜"

30"

2" (TYP)

27"

27"

2"

TOP VIEW

60"

PLACE VELCRO STRIPS HERE (TYP)

¾" DIA DOWEL

2"

¾"

FRONT VIEW

¾"

30"

HANDLE

10 MIL CLEAR PLASTIC

42"

9½"

FILTER MATERIAL

9½"

SIDE VIEW

NOTE: If necessary, change the overall dimensions to fit your workbench.

7

FINISHING THE FINISH

Y̶ou're not quite finished yet. You're close, but you still have a few things to do.

Although you've applied each layer of finish as evenly as possible, and you've sanded between each coat to keep the chemical film flat and smooth, the final finish still isn't what it could be.

To achieve the best possible results, you must rub out the microscopic flaws in the surface and polish it with finer and finer abrasives until it gleams. This is similar to the way jewelers polish jewelry — only your jewel is a hard, resinous film that encases a piece of wood.

After you rub out the finish, you may choose to preserve the surface that you've worked so hard to achieve. By applying a coat of wax or a similar chemical, you can protect the finish from dirt and abrasion and further enhance the look and feel of the wood.

RUBBING OUT A FINISH

Before you can rub out the tiny flaws in the surface, the finish must cure or solidify to a sufficient hardness. This usually takes a great deal more time than it does for a finish to dry between coats. When you applied each new coat of chemicals, you never really gave the preceding coat time to harden completely. There was no need to; in some cases, it might have weakened the *chemical* bond between coats if you had allowed the finish to cure too long.

Furthermore, that sanding you did between coats was not meant to polish the surface. The abrasives were too coarse. They were used primarily to keep the chemical film smooth and even. And by sanding a coarse scratch pattern into a coat of finish, you helped strengthen the *mechanical* bond between it and the next coat.

To polish the surface, however, you must use much finer abrasives. And the finer the abrasive, the harder the finish must be to accept its scratch pattern. You cannot polish a partially cured finish for the same

reason that you cannot sand gelatin. Bits of material come loose, clump together, and load on the sandpaper. Instead of polishing the surface and creating an ultrafine scratch pattern, you end up wiping it with clogged sandpaper.

To properly harden the finish for polishing, there's nothing to do but wait. Finishes vary in the time they take to reach their full hardness. Some, such as lacquer, can be fully hardened in as little as 48 hours. Others, like drying oils or rubbing oils, may require a month or more to cure. If you're unsure how long to wait and the directions on the can give you no clue, consult the chart of "Finish Dry, Set, and Hard Times" below. Or, you can write to the manufacturer. In the time it takes to get an answer, the finish will probably reach a sufficient hardness.

Once the finish cures, you must decide what degree of luster you want — flat, satin, glossy, or somewhere in between. This will determine the type of abrasives you use to polish and how fine they should be.

FINISH DRY, SET, AND HARD TIMES

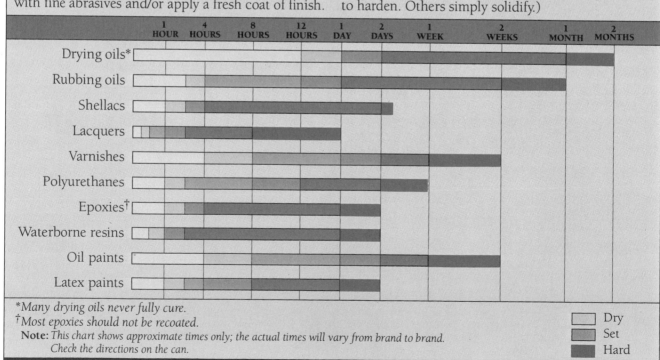

Definition of terms:
- A finish is *dry* when the surface loses its tackiness and dust no longer sticks to it.
- It's *set* when the film is hard enough to sand with fine abrasives and/or apply a fresh coat of finish.
- It's *hard* when the film has solidified completely and is ready to rub to its desired gloss. (Remember, finishes in which a chemical reaction takes place *cure* to harden. Others simply solidify.)

Categories: Drying oils*, Rubbing oils, Shellacs, Lacquers, Varnishes, Polyurethanes, Epoxies†, Waterborne resins, Oil paints, Latex paints

Time scale: 1 HOUR, 4 HOURS, 8 HOURS, 12 HOURS, 1 DAY, 2 DAYS, 1 WEEK, 2 WEEKS, 1 MONTH, 2 MONTHS

Legend: Dry, Set, Hard

*Many drying oils never fully cure.
†Most epoxies should not be recoated.
Note: This chart shows approximate times only; the actual times will vary from brand to brand. Check the directions on the can.

FOR YOUR INFORMATION

You can control luster by using a satin or a glossy finish. But satin finishes contain flatteners, and there is some controversy over whether these additives are necessary or even desirable. Even if you use a satin finish with flatteners, you must polish the surface at least as smooth as a satin luster, or it will look duller than expected. And because flatteners are opaque, they partially obscure the wood grain. For these reasons, many craftsmen choose glossy finishes (without flatteners), then adjust the luster by how they rub out the hardened film.

There are also finishes that you may not want to rub out. For example, a poured epoxy finish, if properly leveled and protected from dust, should look even and glossy with no further help from you. Wipe-on finishes, because they can go on so thin and even, may need nothing more than a protective coat of wax after the last coat. Paint, both oil and latex, rarely needs to be rubbed out. If the finish looks good to you, why mess with it?

INITIAL RUB-OUT — A FLAT FINISH

If the finish does need to be rubbed out, begin by wet sanding it with a slightly finer abrasive than you last used. For example, if you sanded between the coats of finish with 320-grit sandpaper, sand the final finish with 400-grit. Lubricate the paper with a liquid that

won't harm the finish — either water or mineral spirits, whichever is appropriate.

A SAFETY REMINDER

The dust from some hardened finishes can be toxic — epoxy dust is especially dangerous. Wet sanding keeps this dust to a minimum, but wear a dust mask to be safe.

Sand very lightly, especially near the edges. When the finish is still in a liquid state, the surface tension makes it pull away from the arrises and the corners. Consequently, the finish is thinnest at these locations, although you have evened it out somewhat when sanding between coats. Also, the sanding block or sander tends to remove more finish from the arrises and corners than from other surfaces. (SEE FIGURE 7-1.) You must be extra careful when sanding these areas, lest you sand through the finish.

After finishing with one grit, clean the surface and change to a slightly finer grit. You know that it's time to change grits when the luster of the finish on each surface is uniform. When you first start rubbing, the surface will be shiny and uneven. It will become dull and even as you work. Shiny areas indicate low spots or areas where you haven't yet sanded.

Work your way up to 600-grit sandpaper. At this point, the finish will show just a hint of gloss, but it will still be fairly dull and flat. You can stop here, or continue rubbing.

7-1 A sanding block or sander tends to tip as it goes over an edge, and all the sanding pressure is transferred to the arris or corner. If you're not careful, you can cut through the finish in these areas, exposing raw wood. To help prevent this, sand from the center out (rather than from the edges in), and keep the block or sander level.

RUBBING A SATIN OR GLOSS FINISH

If you continue past 600-grit, you have a choice of abrasives. Some craftsmen prefer to go on with wet/dry sandpaper, rubbing with 1000- or even 2000-grit. (These ultrafine paper-backed abrasives are available at most auto supply stores.) Or you can jump to several other abrasives.

The traditional choice is powdered stone — pumice and rottenstone. (*See Figures 7-2 and 7-3.*) Apply these with a felt pad and a sanding block. Rub with 4F pumice for a satin finish, or continue with rottenstone for a glossy look.

You can also use #0000 steel wool: This will give you a luster that's slightly duller than the satin look pumice produces, but not as dull as 600-grit abrasives. Steel wool is especially good for projects with contoured or complex surfaces, since the wool doesn't need to be backed up with a hard, flat block. However, you must be especially careful to rub each surface evenly, or you may go through the finish where it's thin. Lubricate the steel wool with paste wax or a lubricating paste made especially for it. (*See Figure 7-4.*)

Fiberglass abrasive pads, such as Scotch-Brite pads, will do the same job as steel wool. (*See Figure 7-5.*) The *gray* pads are impregnated with a fine silicon carbide abrasive (approximately equal to 320-grit), and will produce a near-satin luster. The *white* pads are covered with talc (approximate equal to 1000-grit), and will create a near-gloss luster. Use water, mineral spirits, or steel wool paste to lubricate the pads when rubbing.

Finally, you can use rubbing compounds (sometimes called *glazes*) that are also used for rubbing out auto paints. These come in many different grits, from 1,000 up to 12,000, for a whole spectrum of lusters, from satin to ultra-super-high gloss. These abrasives are suspended in an inert paste. To use them, spread the paste on a felt-covered sanding block and apply it to the surface as you would pumice or rottenstone. You can also apply rubbing compound with a high-speed polisher. (*See Figures 7-6 and 7-7.*)

For Your Information

If a finish goes on in very thin coats, as rubbing oils and lacquers do, you can sometimes *begin* rubbing them out with #000 or #0000 steel wool. But if the coats are thick, sand first with a sanding block to even out the chemical film.

For Best Results

Rubbing compounds should not be used with open-grain woods when the pores haven't been filled, or on projects with intricate surfaces. The paste works its way into pores and crevices and leaves a light-colored residue.

7-2   To use a powdered stone abrasive, wrap a piece of felt around a sanding block. Dip the felt in water, linseed oil, or paraffin oil, then sprinkle a little powder on the cloth.

7-3   Turn the block over and rub the felt back and forth across the finished surface as if you were sanding. The oil-and-stone mixture should make a creamy paste. Use 4F pumice for a satin finish, then move on to rottenstone for a gloss finish.

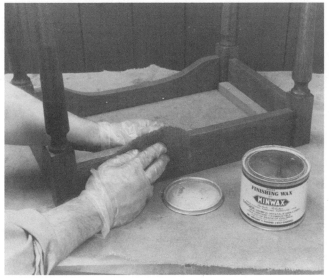

7-4   Ultrafine steel wool will
produce a near-satin luster. When
using steel wool to rub out a finish,
lubricate it with wax or a lubricating
paste made especially for steel wool,
such as Wol-Wax. Just as water or
mineral oil is used for wet/dry sandpaper, wax or paste will float away
the finish dust.

7-5   You can use fiberglass
abrasive pads in place of steel wool.
These wear longer, and you can
clean them with soap and water. The
gray (fine) and white (ultrafine) grits
are available at auto supply stores.

7-6   High-speed polishers and
angle-grinders can speed up the rub-
out chore, especially if you have a lot
of wide, flat surface area. Mount a
buffing pad or bonnet over a hard
rubber backing plate. Apply the rubbing compound to the bonnet, then
swirl the bonnet over the finished
surface. Use the same technique that
you would for hand-rubbing: Work
from the center of each area out
toward the edges. This will prevent
cutting through the finish at the
arrises and corners.

7-7   When using rubbing
compounds, you must work your
way up through the grits just like
sandpaper. To clean one rubbing
compound from a bonnet and
prepare it for another, swirl the bonnet against a piece of scrap wood for
a minute or two.

BUFFING FOR A HIGHER GLOSS

To create a higher gloss finish, continue rubbing with finer and finer abrasives. Or, buff the finish with a polisher and a lamb's-wool bonnet.

Most wood finishes have a *thermoplastic* nature; that is, when you heat them up, they soften and melt. If you heat just the first few layers of molecules on the surface of the chemical film, the finish will flow out, filling all the tiny scratches. Don't make the film too hot or let the heat penetrate to the foundation of the film; if you do, the finish will ball up, bubble, or delaminate from the wood.

A lamb's-wool bonnet, spinning at high speed, creates friction as you hold it against the finish. This friction heats the surface of the chemical film, and if you're very careful you can buff a mirrorlike finish. (*SEE FIGURE 7-8.*)

7-8 As long as a finish has sufficient depth, you can buff it to a very high gloss with a lamb's-wool bonnet mounted on a polisher. You need not use rubbing compound or abrasives of any kind; the friction and the resulting heat will polish the finish. Keep the polisher moving as you buff; be careful not to dwell too long in any one spot.

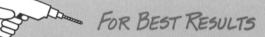

FOR BEST RESULTS

Buffing with a wool bonnet works best on finishes with lots of depth. The thinner the chemical film, the greater the likelihood that you will overheat the finish and cause it to peel up.

PROTECTING A FINISH

After all the work you've done to apply the finish, you may want to protect it. When you begin to use the project, the finish will be subjected to abrasion from dust and dirt, discoloration, the chemical assaults of household cleaners and spilled drinks, and the stress of wood movement. A coat of wax, properly applied and buffed, will help the finish to survive all this wear and tear.

There is controversy over whether or not a finish, if properly applied, requires protection. Certainly some of the hard synthetic finishes, such as epoxy and polyurethane, are durable enough with little need for additional help. And many of the good qualities that wax is popularly thought to bestow are, in fact, old wives' tales. For example, wax does not "feed" or restore a finish, nor does it replenish or replace wood oils.

However, wax *does* add some desirable properties. It lubricates the surface so dust and dirt won't stick, and provides an additional barrier to moisture and certain chemicals. It also fills tiny scratches in the surface, increasing the luster, and gives the finish a pleasant feel and smell.

There are other materials that are commonly used to protect or care for a finish, such as furniture polish and lemon oil. However, none of these are as effective as wax. Many of the chemicals in furniture polish are wax derivatives, but because they are thinned for easy application they do not hold up as well as straight wax. And lemon oil does nothing for a finish except give it a pleasant smell, make it look oily, and turn it into a dust magnet.

FOR YOUR INFORMATION

Despite a popular misconception, lemon oil is *not* intended to be applied directly to a finish. Instead, it's supposed to be sprinkled sparingly on the *dust rag*. This turns the rag into a tack cloth for dust, and dissolves surface grime as you wipe. After a few cleanings, the lemon oil also dissolves the wax and you must rewax the finish.

WAXING THE FINISH

To properly apply a paste wax, you should understand how it works. Like a finish, wax will form a chemical film. However, this film never hardens or cures. Furthermore, wax clings tenaciously to everything *but itself.* After you apply it, you can rub all you want and the wax film, just a few molecules thick, will remain on the surface. But when you apply another coat, it dissolves the first one. Rub it out again and the film will still be only a few molecules thick. No matter how many coats you apply, it will *never* get any thicker — you cannot build up layers of wax as you can finishes.

Apply a thin coat of wax to the finish with a damp cloth. Wait a few minutes for the wax to haze over, then wipe off the excess with a clean cloth. Buff thoroughly with a soft cloth (such as a cotton T-shirt) or a chamois. (*See Figure 7-9.*)

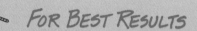

FOR BEST RESULTS

Let the finish harden completely before you apply wax. The wax may interfere with or delay the drying and curing process.

Although it's not necessary, many craftsmen apply two coats of wax to a new project. Although this does not make the wax any thicker or more durable, the second coat helps to cover any areas that might have been missed on the first application.

If you need to remove wax from a surface, dissolve it with naphtha or mineral spirits.

7-9 To apply wax, wipe on a thin layer, let it dry for a few minutes, and wipe off the excess. Then *buff well.* This buffing is very important — if the coat of wax left on the surface is too thick, it will mix with dust and look grimy. You can remove dark, grimy wax simply by applying a fresh coat of clean wax and buffing properly.

Making Your Own Wax

Although there are many types of paste wax available, you can easily mix your own. Most wax formulas contain two or more of these three materials — paraffin, beeswax, and carnauba wax. You can purchase paraffin from a grocery store, and the other two from most finishing suppliers.

Grate the waxes or break them up into chips. (Carnauba usually comes in small flakes.) Mix them in whatever ratio your intuition tells you. Paraffin is the softest (and least expensive) of these ingredients, beeswax is slightly harder, and carnauba is very hard. You want the wax paste to be soft enough to apply and buff out easily, but hard enough to resist wear. Most craftsmen prefer a little bit of carnauba mixed with a lot of paraffin and/or beeswax.

(continued) ▷

MAKING YOUR OWN WAX — CONTINUED

1 **Place the wax chips in a jar** and add just enough turpentine to cover them. Put the lid on the jar and let it sit overnight. When you open the jar the next morning, the turpentine will have dissolved the wax to form an opaque paste.

2 **Because carnauba wax is so** much harder than the others, it may not dissolve completely — especially if the chips are large. If this is the case, gently warm the wax in a double boiler on an electric hot plate until all the ingredients melt into a clear liquid. Turn off the hot plate and let the liquid cool until it resolidifies into a paste. **Warning:** Do *not* heat the wax-and-turpentine mixture over an open flame, or without a double boiler.

3 **Test the consistency of the** mixture. You should be able to spread it on a surface and buff it easily. If it's not easy to spread, add more turpentine. If the paste is not easy to buff, melt it and add more of the soft waxes — paraffin and beeswax. If the paste won't buff to a pleasant shine, melt it and add more carnauba.

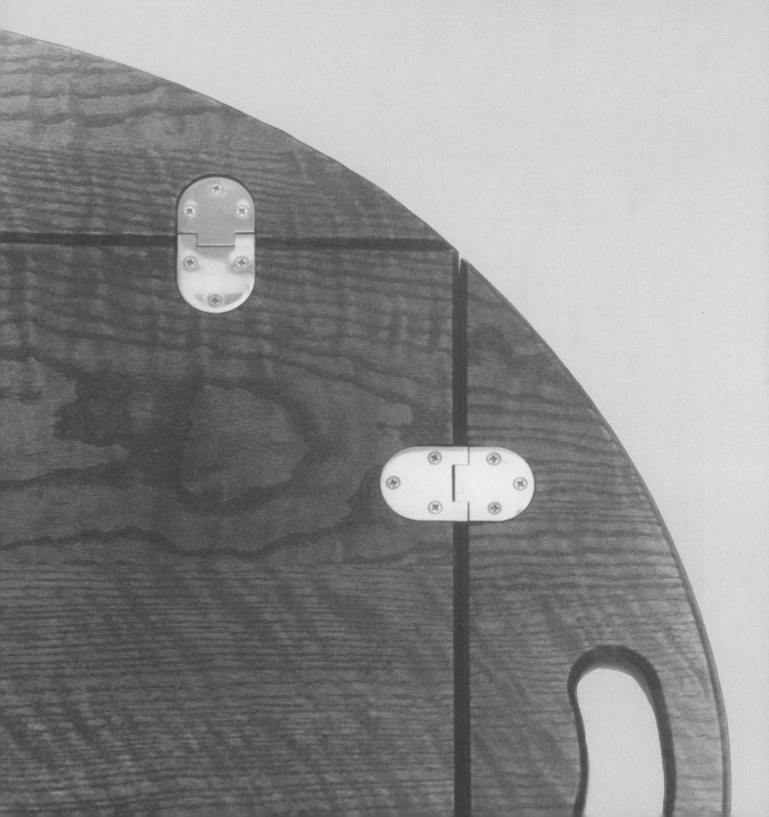

PROJECTS

8

MINIATURE MULE CHEST

Chests have been popular for thousands of years, but have always presented the same problem: How do you retrieve something at the bottom of the chest without sifting through everything on top? You couldn't, until sixteenth century English craftsmen introduced the *mule chest* — a chest with a single "drawing box" (as a drawer was then called) at the bottom.

Later, cabinetmakers added another and another drawer to the design. Eventually, they created a *chest of drawers*. But one-drawer chests remained popular storage pieces for certain items, such as bedding and linens. This miniature mule chest is designed to store jewelry and keepsakes.

The project is stained with a dark cherry aniline dye, then finished with several coats of clear lacquer. The lacquer has been rubbed out with pumice for a satin luster.

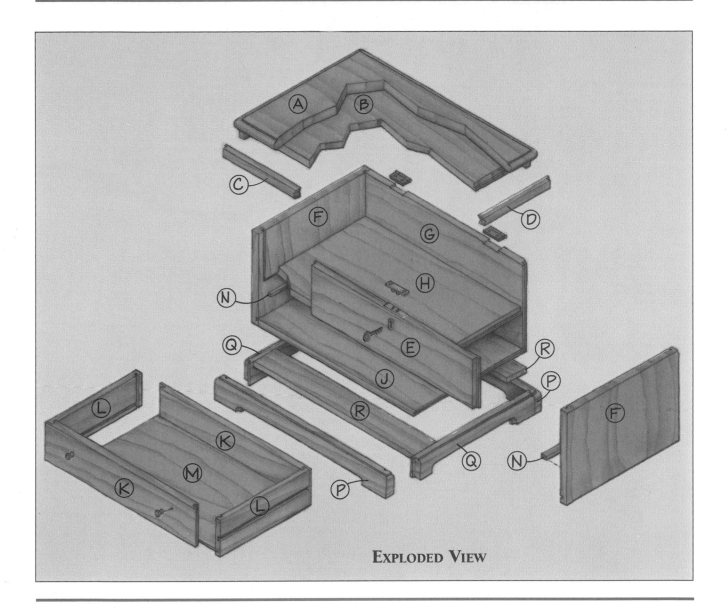

EXPLODED VIEW

MATERIALS LIST (FINISHED DIMENSIONS)

Parts

A. Lid $\frac{1}{2}''$ x $7\frac{1}{4}''$ x $13\frac{7}{8}''$

B. Sub-lid $\frac{3}{8}''$ x $5\frac{1}{2}''$ x $12\frac{5}{8}''$

C. Lid front/
back (2) $\frac{1}{2}''$ x $\frac{5}{8}''$ x $12\frac{5}{8}''$

D. Lid sides (2) $\frac{3}{8}''$ x $\frac{5}{8}''$ x $6\frac{1}{2}''$

E. Front $\frac{1}{2}''$ x $2\frac{3}{8}''$ x $12\frac{5}{8}''$

F. Sides (2) $\frac{3}{8}''$ x $5\frac{1}{4}''$ x $6\frac{1}{2}''$

G. Back $\frac{1}{2}''$ x $5\frac{1}{4}''$ x $12\frac{5}{8}''$

H. Till bottom $\frac{3}{8}''$ x $5\frac{1}{2}''$ x $12\frac{5}{8}''$

J. Bottom $\frac{3}{8}''$ x $6''$ x $12\frac{5}{8}''$

K. Drawer front/
back (2) $\frac{3}{8}''$ x $2\frac{15}{32}''$ x $12\frac{5}{16}''$

L. Drawer
sides (2) $\frac{3}{8}''$ x $2\frac{15}{32}''$ x $5\frac{3}{4}''$

M. Drawer
bottom* $\frac{1}{8}''$ x $5\frac{1}{2}''$ x $11\frac{13}{16}''$

N. Drawer
guides (2) $\frac{1}{4}''$ x $\frac{3}{8}''$ x $5\frac{3}{4}''$

P. Base front/
back (2) $\frac{1}{2}''$ x $1\frac{1}{4}''$ x $13\frac{7}{8}''$

Q. Base sides (2) $\frac{1}{2}''$ x $1\frac{1}{4}''$ x $6\frac{1}{2}''$

R. Ledges (2) $\frac{1}{2}''$ x $1\frac{3}{4}''$ x $12\frac{7}{8}''$

Make this part from plywood.

Hardware

$\frac{1}{2}''$ Drawer pulls (2)

Jewelry box stop hinges and
mounting screws (2)

Jewelry box lock and escutcheon

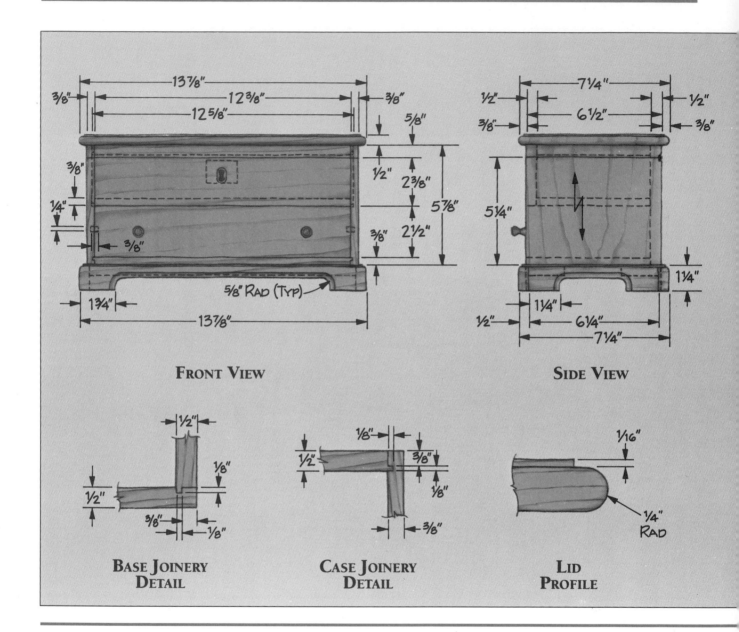

FRONT VIEW

SIDE VIEW

BASE JOINERY
DETAIL

CASE JOINERY
DETAIL

LID
PROFILE

PLAN OF PROCEDURE

1 Select the stock and cut the parts to size.
To build this miniature mule chest, you need about
6 board feet of 4/4 (four-quarters) lumber and a scrap
of 1/8-inch plywood. The chest shown is made from
cherry, but you can use any cabinet-grade hardwood.

Plane all the lumber to 1/2 inch thick and cut all
the 1/2-inch-thick parts to size — front, back, lid, lid
front, lid back, base front, base back, base sides, and
ledges. Set aside a small amount of 1/2-inch-thick
stock to use for test pieces, then plane the remaining
stock to 3/8 inch thick. Cut all the 3/8-inch-thick parts
to size *except* the sides, lid sides, and drawer parts.

Cut two 6 1/2-inch-wide, 6-inch-long boards for the
sides and lid sides, as shown in the *Side/Lid Side
Layout*. Don't cut the drawer front, back, sides, or bottom yet — wait until you've built the case. However,
you can rip 1/4-inch-wide strips of the 3/8-inch-thick
stock to make the drawer guides.

2 Rout the joinery in the sides. Lay out the
dadoes and grooves on the boards you have cut to
make the sides and lid sides, as shown in the *Side/Lid
Side Layout*. Also, lay out the dadoes in the base front
and back, as shown in the *Base Joinery Detail*. Cut

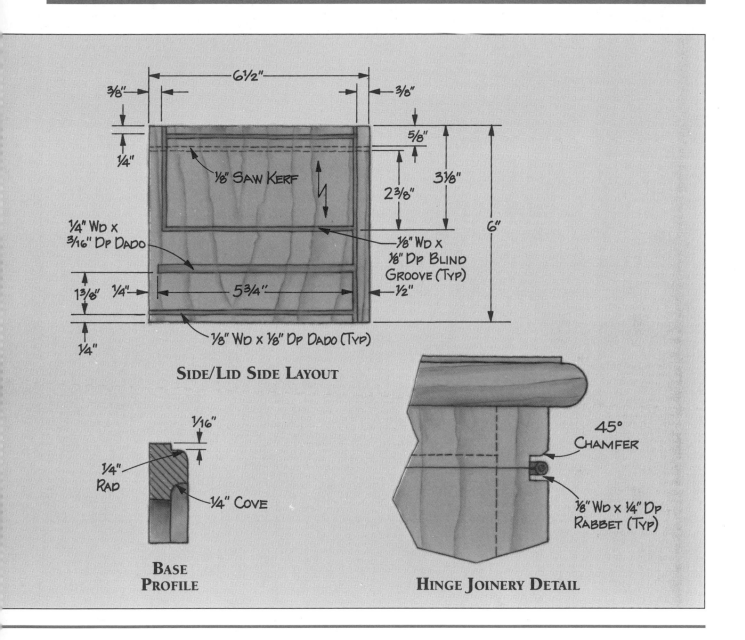

SIDE/LID SIDE LAYOUT

6½"

3/8"

3/8"

¼"

5/8"

⅛" SAW KERF

3⅛"

2⅜"

¼" WD x
3/16" DP DADO

⅛" WD x
⅛" DP BLIND
GROOVE (TYP)

6"

1⅜"

¼"

5¾"

½"

¼"

⅛" WD x ⅛" DP DADO (TYP)

**BASE
PROFILE**

1/16"

¼"
RAD

¼" COVE

45°
CHAMFER

⅛" WD x ¼" DP
RABBET (TYP)

HINGE JOINERY DETAIL

these joints with a router and a straight bit. Saw the side boards in two to make the sides and lid sides.

3 Cut tongues to fit the grooves and dadoes. The ends of the front, back, till bottom, bottom, lid front, lid back, and base sides are all rabbeted. These rabbets create tongues that fit the dadoes or grooves, as shown in the *Case Joinery Detail* and *Base Joinery Detail*. Cut the rabbets with a dado cutter or table-mounted router. Also rabbet the edges of the back and lid back, as shown in the *Hinge Joinery Detail*. Chamfer the outside arris of the lid back rabbet.

4 Cut and shape the base parts. Lay out the cutouts in the base front, base back, and base sides, as shown in the *Front View* and *Side View*. Make these cutouts with a band saw or scroll saw, then sand the sawed edges. Using a table-mounted router and cove bit, rout coves in the outside edges of the cutouts.

5 Mortise the front for a lock. Lay out the mortise for the lock on the inside surface of the front. Rough out the mortise with a router and a straight bit, then square the corners with a chisel. Also, drill a keyhole through the front and elongate it with a file.

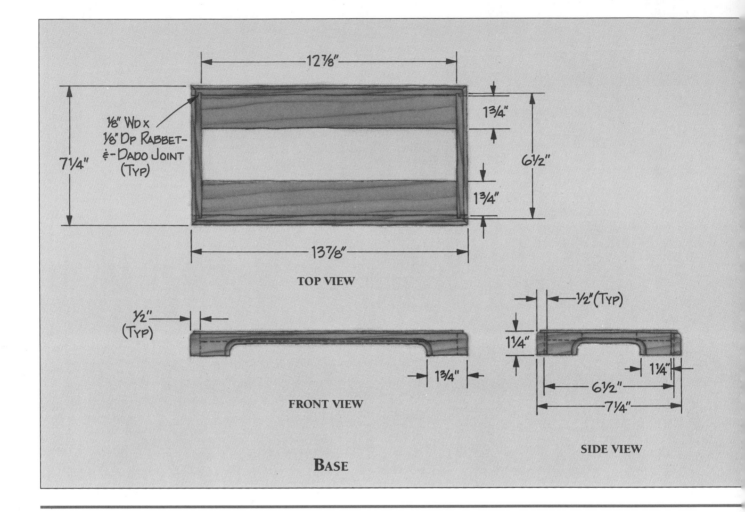

1/8" WD x 1/8" DP RABBET-&-DADO JOINT (TYP)

12 7/8"

7 1/4"

1 3/4"

6 1/2"

1 3/4"

13 7/8"

TOP VIEW

1/2" (TYP)

1 3/4"

FRONT VIEW

1/2" (TYP)

1 1/4"

1 1/4"

6 1/2"

7 1/4"

SIDE VIEW

BASE

Make sure that the lock fits the mortise, and that the key and escutcheon fit the hole. But don't install the hardware yet.

6   Assemble the case and base.   Finish sand all the parts that you have completed so far. Glue together the front, back, sides, drawer guides, bottom, and till bottom to make the case. Glue the sublid, lid front, lid back, and lid sides together to make the lid assembly. Glue the base front, base back, base sides, and ledges together to make the base. Let the glue dry, then sand all the joints clean and flush.

7   Shape the edges of the lid and base.   Using a table-mounted router and a roundover bit, shape the edges of the lid and the top edges of the assembled base, as shown in the *Lid Profile* and *Base Profile*.

8   Attach the lid and base.   Finish sand the routed edges of the lid and base. Then glue the lid to

the lid assembly and the base to the case. Cut mortises in the lid and case assemblies for hinges. Attach the hinges to the lid, then attach the lid to the case.

Install the lock and escutcheon in the front. Close the lid, mark where the lid front meets the lock, and mortise the lid front for the catch. Install the catch, making sure that it "marries" the lock properly.

9   Cut and join the drawer parts.   Measure the drawer opening in the case. If the measurements differ from the drawings, make the necessary adjustments in the dimensions of the drawer parts. Cut the drawer front, back, sides, and bottom to size. **Note:** As shown in the *Drawer/Top View, Drawer/Front View,* and *Drawer/Side View,* the drawer is slightly smaller than the opening. Note that you can make drawers the *same size* as their openings, then plane or sand them to fit.

Like the lid, case, and base, the drawer is assembled with dadoes and grooves. Rout these joints with a

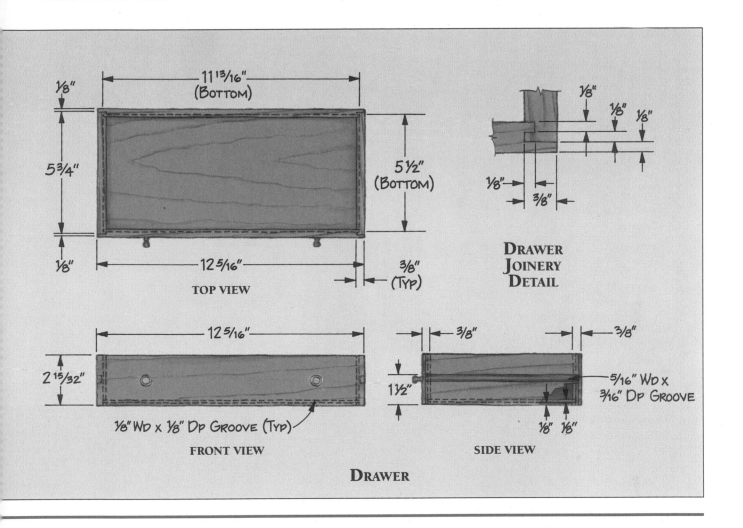

1/8"
11 13/16"
(BOTTOM)

5 3/4"

5 1/2"
(BOTTOM)

1/8"

12 5/16"

3/8"
(TYP)

TOP VIEW

**DRAWER
JOINERY
DETAIL**

1/8"
1/8"
1/8"

1/8"
3/8"

12 5/16"

3/8"   3/8"

2 15/32"

1 1/2"

5/16" WD x
3/16" DP GROOVE

1/8" WD x 1/8" DP GROOVE (TYP)

1/8" 1/8"

FRONT VIEW   **SIDE VIEW**

DRAWER

router and straight bits. You can make the lock joint shown in the *Drawer Joinery Detail* with a single setup on a table-mounted router. (*SEE FIGURES 8-1 THROUGH 8-3.*) Also cut grooves in the inside faces of the drawer parts to hold the drawer bottom, and in the outside faces of the drawer sides to fit the drawer guides.

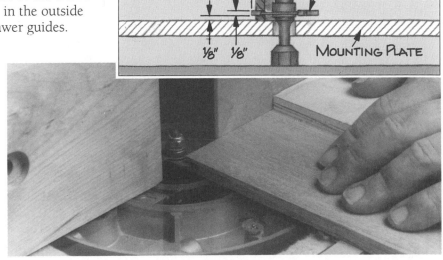

REMOVABLE SPACER   FENCE

1/4"

3/8"   SPLINE CUTTER

1/8" 1/8"   MOUNTING PLATE

8-1 Make a ¹/₄-inch spacer from plywood or hardboard, then set up the router and the spline cutter as shown in the inset. Remove the spacer and cut a ¹/₈-inch-wide, ³/₈-inch-deep groove in the ends of each drawer front and back. This groove will create two ¹/₈-inch-thick tenons in each end.

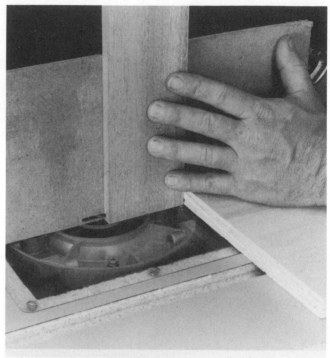

8-2 Clamp the spacer to the router table fence. Holding the drawer fronts and backs vertically against the spacer, cut the *inside* tenons so they're just ⅛ inch long.

8-3 Finally, cut a ⅛-inch-wide, ⅛-inch-deep dado in the inside surface of each drawer side, near each end. Again, hold each part vertically as you make the cuts. When you fit the joints together, the short tenons on the drawer fronts and backs should fit the dadoes in the drawer sides.

10 Assemble and fit the drawer. Finish sand the drawer parts, then assemble the front, back, and sides with glue. Slide the drawer bottom into place as you assemble the other parts, but don't glue it — let it float in the grooves. When the glue is dry, sand the drawer joints clean and flush.

Install the pulls on the drawer front. Fit the drawer to the opening, inserting the drawer guides in the side grooves. The drawer should slide in and out of the case without binding. If it binds, scrape or sand the drawer parts until it slides easily.

11 Finish the completed chest. Although you can apply any finish that suits your fancy, the chest shown was stained with aniline dye and sprayed with lacquer. To duplicate this finish, use the following schedule:

■ Remove the drawer and lid from the case, then detach the hardware and set it aside. Sand all wood surfaces to 180-grit, then clean with a tack cloth.

■ Stain the wood with a dark water-soluble aniline dye. Let dry overnight.

■ If necessary, fill the wood pores with a dark filler or several coats of sealer. The chest shown is made from cherry, which has fairly small pores. To fill these, apply a coat of sanding sealer, sand lightly, wipe down with a tack cloth, and repeat.

■ Spray on the lacquer primer or base coat. Let dry until sufficiently hard for sanding, then sand with wet/dry 400-grit sandpaper, lubricating the paper with mineral spirits. Wipe the sanded surface down with a tack cloth.

■ Spray on the first coat of lacquer, let dry, and sand with 400-grit sandpaper.

■ Spray on a second coat of lacquer and let dry overnight. Let the finish harden completely, then sand with 600-grit sandpaper.

■ Rub out the finish with pumice.

■ Apply a coat of paste wax and buff well.

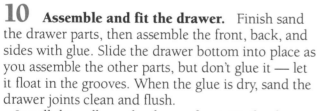

9

Step-Back Cupboard

During the eighteenth and nineteenth centuries, no American kitchen was complete without a *cupboard* — a set of shelves enclosed by doors, which stored food and dishes. One of the most popular styles was this tall "step-back" cupboard, consisting of a wide base, a work surface, and a shallow top. This arrangement provided both storage and a work area in the same space, and later evolved into the built-in kitchen cabinets that grace most contemporary kitchens.

The simple lines of this particular step-back cupboard are reminiscent of many "country" pieces — modest, utilitarian furniture built by early American craftsmen for common folks. Although it's a new cupboard, this piece is finished so that it looks like an early nineteenth-century antique. The raw wood was chemically treated to create an artificial patina, and covered with two colors of milk paint. The paint was then distressed and glazed to imitate years of wear and tear.

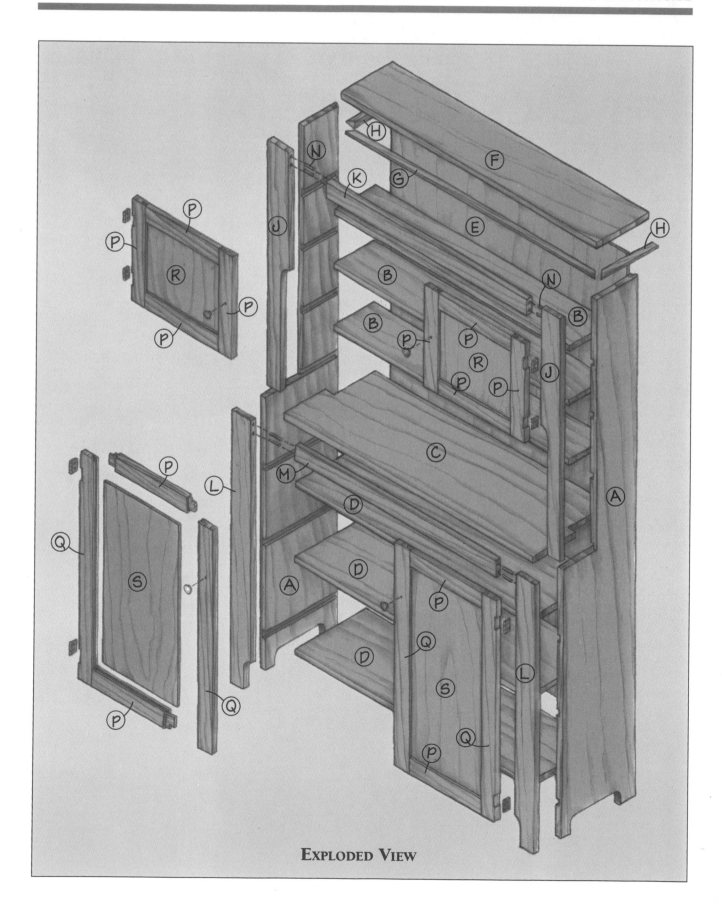

EXPLODED VIEW

MATERIALS LIST (FINISHED DIMENSIONS)

Parts

A. Sides (2) $3/4''$ x $11''$ x $67^3/4''$

B. Top
   shelves (3) $3/4''$ x $5^3/4''$ x $35^1/4''$

C. Counter $3/4''$ x $12^1/4''$ x $37^1/2''$

D. Bottom
   shelves (3) $3/4''$ x $10^3/4''$ x $35^1/4''$

E. Back* $1/4''$ x $35^1/4''$ x $64^1/8''$

F. Top $3/4''$ x $8^1/4''$ x $39''$

G. Front top
   trim $3/4''$ x $3/4''$ x $37^1/2''$

H. Side top
   trim (2) $3/4''$ x $3/4''$ x $7^1/2''$

J. Top face frame
   stiles (2) $3/4''$ x $3''$ x $31^3/4''$

K. Top face
   frame rail $3/4''$ x $2^3/4''$ x $30''$

L. Bottom face frame
   stiles (2) $3/4''$ x $3''$ x $35^1/4''$

M. Bottom face
   frame rail $3/4''$ x $2''$ x $30''$

N. Dowels (8) $3/8''$ dia. x $2''$

P. Top door stiles/door
   rails (12) $3/4''$ x $2''$ x $12^{15}/16''$

Q. Bottom door
   stiles (4) $3/4''$ x $2''$ x $29^3/16''$

R. Top door
   panels* (2) $1/4''$ x $11^5/8''$ x $9^5/8''$

S. Bottom door
   panels* (2) $1/4''$ x $11^5/8''$ x $25^7/8''$

*Make these parts from plywood.

Hardware

$1^1/2''$ x $2^1/2''$ Butt hinges and
   mounting screws (8)

$1^1/2''$ Door pulls (4)

Door catches and mounting
   screws (4)

$1''$ Wire brads (20–24)

4d Finishing nails (16–20)

PLAN OF PROCEDURE

1 Select the stock and cut the parts to size. To make this project, you need approximately 40 board feet of 4/4 (four-quarters) lumber, and one 4- by 8-foot sheet of $1/4$-inch plywood. The cupboard shown is made from a variety of woods. In fact, many of the pieces were scraps — there was no need to use matching materials since the cupboard was going to be painted. If you don't want to paint your cupboard, use a cabinet-grade wood and a plywood with a matching veneer.

Plane all the 4/4 lumber to $3/4$ inch thick, then cut all the parts to size *except* the top moldings and door parts. Set aside some stock that's at least 2 inches wide to make the moldings. Don't cut any of the door parts until after you've built the case.

2 Cut the joinery in the sides and top. The case is assembled with simple rabbets and dadoes. Lay out the joints on the sides and top, as shown in the *Side Layout* and *Top Layout.* Cut these with a dado cutter or hand-held router. Note that the rabbet on the back edge of the top is blind at both ends — it's stopped $1^7/8$ inch from either end of the board. The easiest way to make a blind rabbet is to cut it with a router, then square the blind ends with a chisel.

3 Cut the shapes of the sides, counter, and face frame stiles. Lay out the shapes of the sides as shown in the *Side Layout,* the counter as shown in the *Counter Layout,* and the face frame stiles as shown in the *Front View.* Cut the shapes with a band saw or saber saw, then sand the sawed edges.

4 Drill dowel holes in the face frame parts. The face frame rails are attached to the stiles with dowels. Using a doweling jig, drill holes for these dowels. Test the fit of the dowel joints, but do *not* glue up the face frames yet. **Note:** If you wish, you can also use biscuits or mortise-and-tenon joints to join the frame members.

5 Assemble the case. Finish sand the case parts, being careful not to round-over adjoining surfaces. When sanding the shelves, don't reduce the *thickness* where they fit in the dadoes. You may want to use masking tape to protect surfaces you don't want to sand.

Assemble the sides, shelves, and counter with glue. Fasten the top to the sides with glue and finishing nails, then attach the back to the sides, top, and shelves with brads. Join the face frame members with dowels and glue, and glue the assembled frames to the case. Let the glue dry, then drive finishing nails down through the counter and into the sides and bottom face frame. Set the heads of the nails and brads, and sand all joints clean and flush.

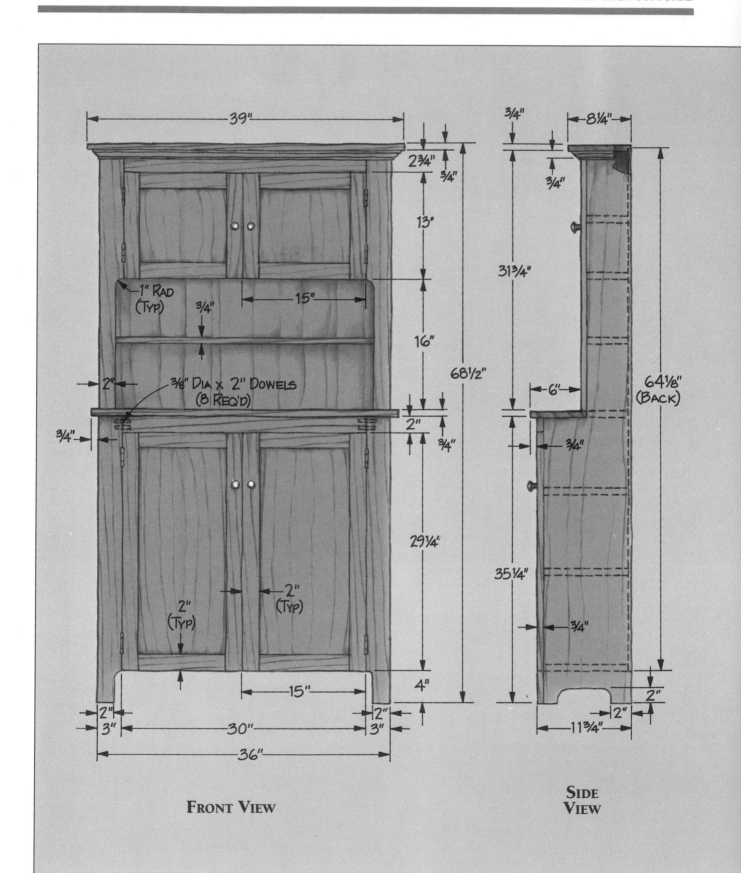

39"
2¾"
¾"
13"
15"
¾"
16"
1" RAD (TYP)
2"
⅜" DIA x 2" DOWELS (8 REQ'D)
68½"
¾"
2"
¾"
29¼"
2" (TYP)
2" (TYP)
15"
4"
2"
3"
30"
3"
36"

FRONT VIEW

¾"
8¼"
¾"
31¾"
6"
64⅛" (BACK)
¾"
¾"
35¼"
¾"
2"
2"
11¾"

SIDE VIEW

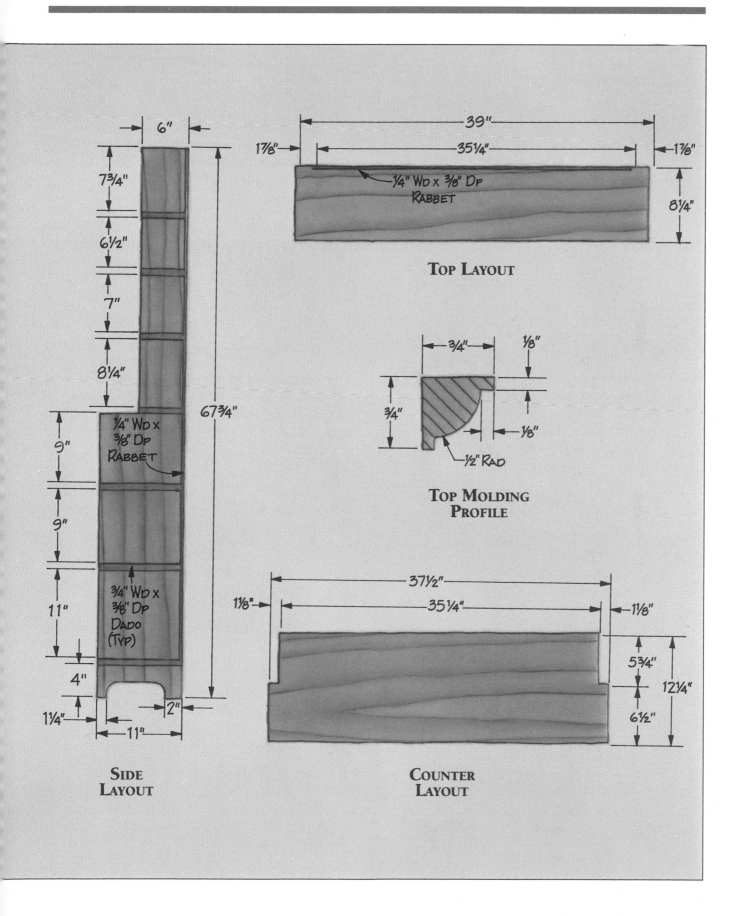

6"

7¾"

6½"

7"

8¼"

67¾"

¼" WD x
⅜" DP
RABBET

9"

9"

¾" WD x
⅜" DP
DADO
(TYP)

11"

4"

1¼"

2"

11"

SIDE
LAYOUT

39"

1⅞"

35¼"

1⅞"

¼" WD x ⅜" DP
RABBET

8¼"

TOP LAYOUT

¾"

⅛"

¾"

⅛"

½" RAD

TOP MOLDING
PROFILE

37½"

1⅛"

35¼"

1⅛"

5¾"

12¼"

6½"

COUNTER
LAYOUT

6 Make and fit the top molding. Using a router or shaper, cut a ½-inch quarter-round bead in one edge of the top molding stock, as shown in the *Top Molding Profile*. Rip the ¾-inch-wide molding from the board. **Warning:** Do not rout or shape narrow stock. It may come apart in your hands.

After shaping and ripping the molding, cut it to length, mitering the adjoining ends. Attach the front top molding to the case with glue and finishing nails. Glue the mitered ends of the side moldings to the front moldings, but do *not* glue the side moldings to the case. The grain direction of the sides and top runs perpendicular to the side moldings. If you glue the moldings in place, they will prevent the case parts from expanding and contracting with changes in humidity. Eventually, the sides and top will warp or split. Instead, fasten the side moldings to the sides and top with finishing nails *only*. Set the heads of the nails.

7 Assemble the doors. Measure the door openings in the assembled case. If they are different from the measurements shown on the drawings, make the necessary adjustments in the dimensions of the door parts. Cut the door rails, stiles, and panels to size. **Note:** As shown in the *Top Door Layout* and *Bottom Door Layout*, the doors are slightly smaller than their openings. Many craftsmen prefer to make doors the same size as their openings, then sand or plane them to get a good fit.

The door frames are assembled with haunched mortises and tenons, as shown in the *Door Frame Joinery Detail*, while the panels rest in grooves in the inside edges of the frame members. Cut these grooves first, using a dado cutter or router. (*SEE FIGURE 9-1.*) Rout or drill mortises in the stiles, near the ends. (*SEE FIGURE 9-2.*) Cut tenons in the ends of the rails to fit the mortises, then cut a notch in one edge of each tenon to create a haunch. (*SEE FIGURES 9-3 AND 9-4.*)

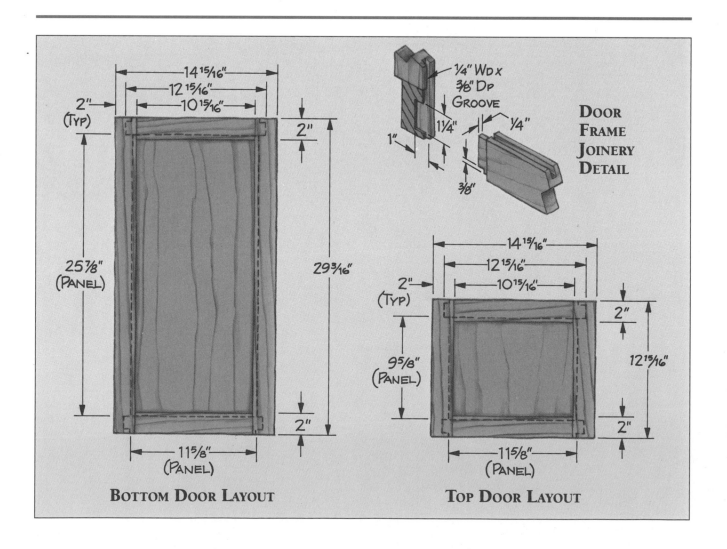

BOTTOM DOOR LAYOUT

TOP DOOR LAYOUT

9-1 Using a dado cutter or a table-mounted router, cut ¼-inch-wide, ⅜-inch-deep grooves in the *inside* edges of the door rails and stiles. These grooves must be perfectly centered in the edges.

9-2 Drill or rout ¼-inch-wide, 1¼-inch long, 1-inch-deep mortises in the stiles, ⅜ inch from each end. The sides of the mortises must be flush with the sides of the grooves. Square the ends of the mortises and trim the sides (if necessary) with a chisel.

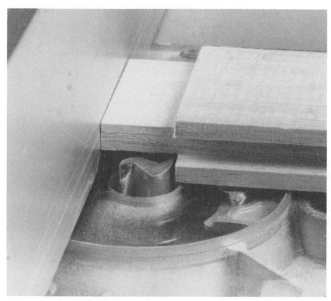

9-3 Rout or cut ¼-inch-thick, 1-inch-long tenons on the ends of the rails. These tenons must fit the mortises snugly, but not too tightly.

9-4 Cut a ⅜-inch-wide, ⅝-inch-long notch in one edge of each tenon. This will create a ⅜-inch step or "haunch" in the tenon. When the joint is assembled, the narrow part of the tenon fits into the mortise, and the haunch fits into the groove.

Lightly sand the door parts. Assemble the frames with glue, fitting the tenons into the mortises. As you do so, slip the panels into the grooves. Do *not* glue the panels in place; they should float in the assembled door frames. Let the glue dry and install the pulls.

8 Fit and hang the doors. Place the case on its back, then rest the doors on the edges of the shelves. Sand or plane the edges until they fit properly. There should be a small gap — $\frac{1}{32}$ to $\frac{1}{16}$ inch wide — between each door and its neighboring parts.

Wedge the doors in the frame with scraps of wood, toothpicks, or cardboard. Mark the locations of the hinges on both the door frames and the face frames. Remove the doors and cut the hinge mortises. Install the hinges on the doors, then hang the doors in the case. Also install the door catches.

9 Finish the cupboard. Although you can apply any type of finish, the cupboard shown was painted with homemade milk paint and artificially aged to imitate an antique. To duplicate the finish shown, follow this finishing schedule:

■ Remove the doors from the cupboard and the hardware from the doors. Lightly sand all wood surfaces to 150-grit, then clean the surfaces with a tack cloth.

■ Apply a 20 percent solution of nitric acid to all wood surfaces, inside and out, then neutralize it with household ammonia. (Refer to "Applying a Chemical Stain" on page 54.) This will stain the wood a darker color, imitating an old patina. As an alternative, you can stain the wood with a dark brown water-soluble aniline dye. It's not important that the stain be com-

pletely even, but it should penetrate as deeply as possible. Let the cupboard dry overnight.

■ Apply a base coat of milk paint. You can either mix your own, or apply a commercial paint. (Refer to "Reproducing Antique Finishes" on page 24.) Paint the inside of the cupboard white or a light cream color — the insides of old-time cabinets were often whitewashed to make it easier to see what was in them. However, you can paint the outside any color you wish. Let the paint dry overnight.

■ Lightly sand the base coat, cutting through the paint to expose the wood in those areas where you would expect to see the most wear — the feet, fronts of shelves, surfaces around the pulls. Clean the surfaces with a tack cloth.

■ Apply a second coat of paint over the first. The color should *contrast* that of the first coat. Let the paint dry overnight.

■ Again, sand through the paint, exposing the base coat beneath it in some areas. In the areas that would show the most wear, sand down to the raw wood.

■ Lightly distress the surface by beating it a few times with two dozen or so keys wired together. (*SEE FIGURE 9-5.*) Don't overdo this! Also, round-over the edges that would wear most with a rasp or file.

■ Apply a brown glaze to all the painted and wooden surfaces. Let the glaze sit a few moments, giving it time to soak into the wood. Then wipe as much glaze as possible off the surface with a clean towel. Let the glaze remain on the raw wood, or wherever it has soaked into a crevice or distress mark.

■ To add gloss to the milk paint finish, apply one or more coats of varnish after the glaze has hardened.

9-5 To imitate wear and tear on the surface of a project, attach 20 to 30 old keys to a short wooden handle. Beat the surface several times with the keys to make gouges and scratches. Be careful not to beat too hard or too long — the surface should look well used, but not as if it has been through a war.

10

KNIFE BLOCK AND CUTTING BOARD

Most knife blocks hold only knives. This particular design, however, holds both knives *and* a cutting board. It's more practical to keep them in the same location — you rarely use one without the other.

The design is as versatile as it is practical. You can adapt the size and shape of the block to hold as many or as few knives as you want. You can also change the design of the cutting board to suit your needs. The block, with the cutting board and knives in place, will rest on a counter or hang on a wall.

Both the knife block and the cutting board are protected by non-toxic finishes. The block is coated with a penetrating salad bowl finish, an inert, nonpoisonous formula that will not flake off or leach out of the wood. The cutting board has been brushed with hot paraffin wax, making it watertight.

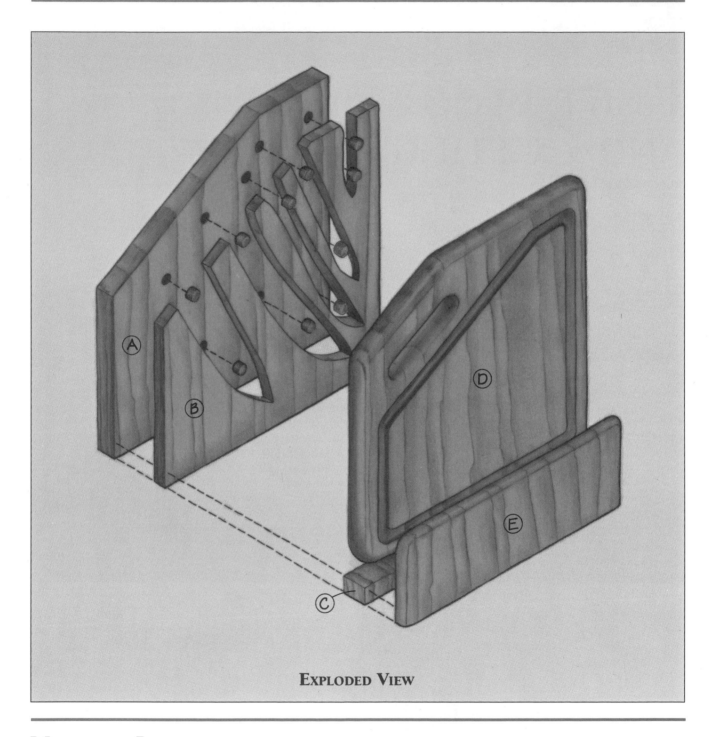

EXPLODED VIEW

MATERIALS LIST (FINISHED DIMENSIONS)

Parts

A. Back   ³⁄₄″ x (variable) x (variable)

B. Knife holder ½″ x (variable) x (variable)

C. Spacer   ³⁄₄″ x 1″ x (variable)

D. Cutting board 1″ x (variable) x (variable)

E. Front   ½″ x 3¹⁄₄″ x (variable)

Hardware

½″-dia. Magnetic disks (2–3 per knife)

Set of knives

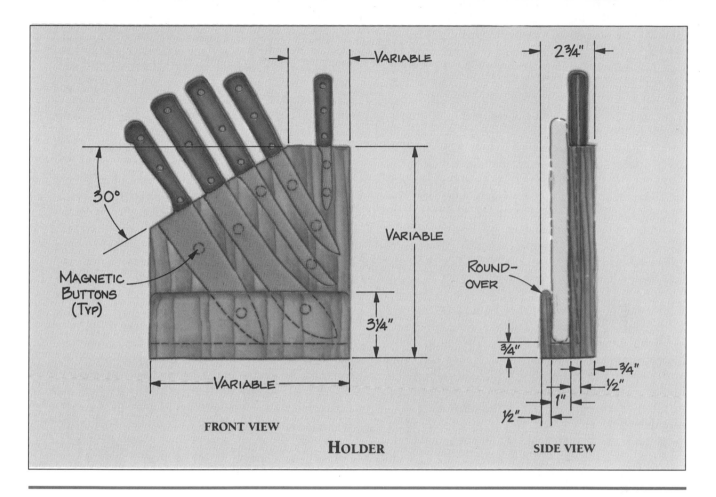

MAGNETIC BUTTONS (TYP)

30°

VARIABLE

VARIABLE

3¼"

VARIABLE

FRONT VIEW

HOLDER

2¾"

ROUND-OVER

¾"

¾"

½"

1"

½"

SIDE VIEW

PLAN OF PROCEDURE

1 Calculate the dimensions of the knife block and cutting board. The width and height of the knife block and the cutting board will depend on the knives that you wish to store. To figure these dimensions, place a piece of paper on the workbench. Arrange your knife set on this paper in the positions that you want to store them. Place the two knives that you use the most on either end — this will make them easier to slip in and out of the block.

Trace the outlines of the knives on the paper, then remove the knives and draw the outline of the knife block. The top edge of the knife block should align with the bottom edges of the knife handles — only the blades should rest inside the block. You can make the block's top edge horizontal, angled, or part horizontal and part angled (as shown). You may have to make several arrangements and drawings until you find a design that works practically and aesthetically. When you've finished arranging and drawing, measure the width and height of the outline.

2 Select the stock and cut the parts to size. Unless your knife set is very large, you'll need only a small amount (less than 3 board feet) of wood to make this project. And because all the parts are fairly small, you may be able to make it from scraps. Be careful what species of wood you use for the cutting board — it should be fairly hard in order to resist damage from the knives, and it should have a closed grain to inhibit vegetable and meat juices from penetrating. Maple, birch, cherry, and the harder varieties of basswood all work well. The cutting board shown is made from maple.

When you have selected the stock, plane it to the thicknesses required and cut all the parts to the sizes needed. Remember, the grain direction of the back, knife holder, spacer, and front must all be *parallel* when assembled so they will all expand and contract in the same direction.

3 Cut the shapes of the back, knife holder, and cutting board. Since the shape of the back and the knife holder are the same, you can cut both parts in one operation. Stick the back and the knife holder together face to face with double-faced carpet tape. Make sure the ends and edges are flush. Lay out the shape of these parts on one of the exposed faces, then cut the shape with a table saw or band saw. Sand the sawed edges, separate the parts, and discard the tape.

Lay out the shape of the cutting board on the stock. Cut the outside shape with a table saw or band saw. To make the cutout for the handle, drill two 1-inch-diameter holes 3¼ inches apart, as shown on the *Cutting Board Layout.* Remove the waste between the holes with a coping saw, scroll saw, or saber saw. Sand the sawed edges.

4 Rout a groove in the cutting board. As shown in the *Cutting Board Layout,* one side of the cutting board has a ½-inch-wide, round-bottom groove that runs around the perimeter. The purpose of this groove is to collect meat or vegetable juice from the food as you cut it, and to keep it from spilling onto the counter. This groove is cut with a router, a ⅝-inch-diameter guide collar, and a ½-inch-diameter veining bit. But before you can rout the groove, you must make a template to guide the router.

The template is simply a scrap of wood or plywood cut to the same shape as the groove you want to rout. Choose a scrap that's slightly thicker than the guide collar is long. Lay out the shape of the groove on this scrap. To compensate for the difference in diameters between the guide collar and the bit, make the template shape ⅛ inch narrower and shorter than the shape you want to rout. Cut the template shape with

a band saw or scroll saw and sand the sawed edges.

Stick the template to the *outside* face of the cutting board (the side that will be turned away from the knives when the cutting board is stored). Adjust the router's depth of cut so when the router is resting on the template, the bit will cut ¼ inch into the cutting board. Rout the groove, keeping the guide collar pressed against the template as you cut. *(SEE FIGURE 10-1.)*

5 Cut the recesses for the knives in the knife holder. Lay the knives on one face of the knife holder and arrange them in the same positions that you will store them. Trace the outlines of the blades, then cut the outlines with a band saw or scroll saw. Sand the sawed edges. Check that the knives fit the recesses you have made.

6 Install the magnetic disks in the back. The knives are held in the knife holder by ½-inch-diameter magnetic disks, inlaid in the back. To lay out the positions of the disks, rest the knife holder on the back and trace the shape of the knife cutouts. Remove the knife holder, then arrange the magnetic disks inside the cutout outlines. Use two disks per knife, placing one disk near the tip and the other near the handle. (**Note:** If a knife is unusually large or heavy, it may require three magnets.) Trace the location of the disks.

Measure the thickness of the magnetic disks. Drill stopped ½-inch-diameter holes for the disks in the back, making each as deep as the disks are thick. Using epoxy glue, install the disks in the back so the disk faces are flush with the wood surface. Let the epoxy harden, then sand off any excess glue.

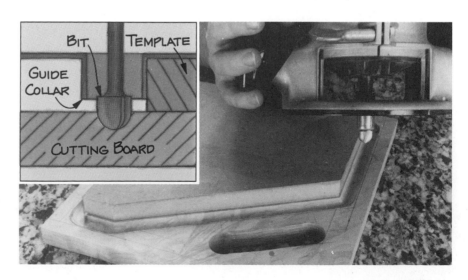

10-1 To rout the round-bottom groove in the cutting board, attach a guide collar to the router sole and a wooden template to the cutting board. Rest the router on the template face, keeping the guide collar pressed against the template edge. Feed the router *counterclockwise* around the template, following the shape with the guide collar.

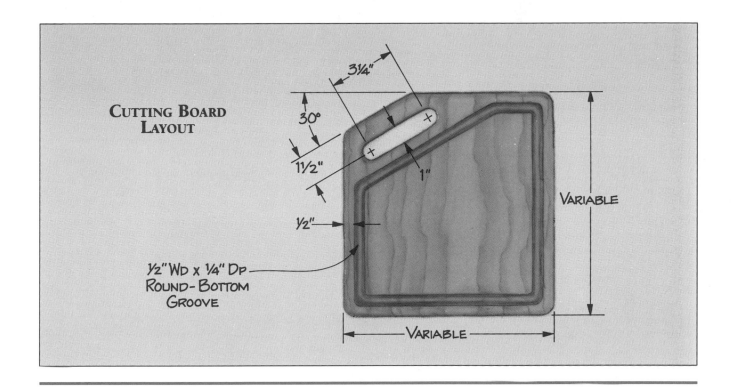

CUTTING BOARD LAYOUT

3¼"

30°

1½"

1"

VARIABLE

½"

VARIABLE

½" WD x ¼" DP ROUND-BOTTOM GROOVE

WHERE TO FIND IT

You can purchase ceramic magnetic disks from the following sources:

Edmund Scientific Company
101 East Gloucester Pike
Barrington, NJ 08007

Meisel Hardware Specialties
P.O. Box 70
Mound, MN 55364

7 Assemble the knife block. Finish sand the back, knife holder, spacer, and front, being careful not to round-over the adjoining surfaces. Laminate these parts face to face with waterproof resorcinol or epoxy glue. As mentioned previously, the grain direction of all four parts must be *parallel*.

Rough sand the cutting board, removing enough stock to make it a little thinner than the spacer. When the cutting board slides easily in and out of the assembled knife block, finish sand it.

8 Apply a finish to the knife block and cutting board. Do any necessary touch-up sanding to the knife block and cutting board. You can apply your choice of nontoxic finishes to the wooden surfaces,

but to duplicate the finish shown, follow this finishing schedule:

■ Wipe two or three coats of salad bowl finish on the knife block, letting each coat dry for several hours before applying the next.

■ Let the last coat of salad bowl finish cure for at least two days. Rub out the finish with paste wax and #0000 steel wool, then buff with a clean cloth.

■ Using a double boiler and an electric hot plate, melt about 2 or 3 ounces of paraffin wax. Gently warm the surface of the cutting board with a heat gun or hair dryer. While a helper continues to blow warm air on the wood surface, brush the wax on the cutting board.

■ Keep warming the cutting board for 5 to 10 minutes, letting the liquid wax penetrate the wood.

■ Before the wax cools and hardens, wipe off any excess that hasn't soaked into the wood.

■ Let the cutting board cool to room temperature, then buff the wax.

FOR YOUR INFORMATION

Although paraffin wax provides an effective barrier to moisture, it's not a durable finish. It should be replenished about once a year.

MAKING YOUR OWN KNIVES

If you wish, you can make your own set of kitchen knives by riveting wooden handles to metal knife blanks. The set shown consists of a paring knife, a boner or utility knife, a carving knife, a butcher's knife, and a chef's or French knife. Depending on the kind of cooking you do, you may wish to add a bread knife, cleaver, or other cutting utensils.

You can buy blanks, rivets, and other knife-making supplies from:
Koval Supplies
460 D Schrock Road
Columbus, OH 43226
Once you have selected the blanks, attach handles that match or complement the knife block.

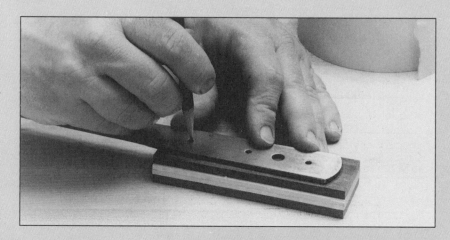

1 **Plane the stock so the knife** handle will be ¾ to 1 inch thick when installed. Cut the handle stock into blocks slightly wider and longer than needed. Stack these blocks *as you will install them,* sticking them together with double-faced carpet tape. Using the metal knife blank as a template, trace the shape of the handle and the positions of the rivet holes onto the face of one block.

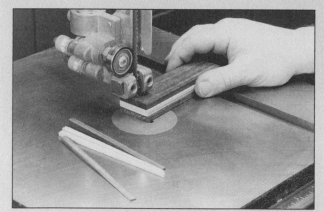
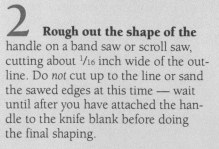

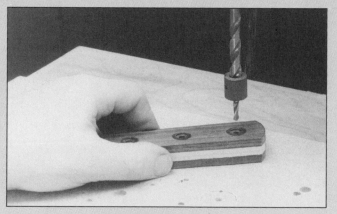

2 **Rough out the shape of the** handle on a band saw or scroll saw, cutting about ¹/₁₆ inch wide of the outline. Do *not* cut up to the line or sand the sawed edges at this time — wait until after you have attached the handle to the knife blank before doing the final shaping.

3 **Drill a ¹/₁₆-inch-diameter** hole through the stacked handle stock at each rivet hole location. This will transfer the locations to the unmarked side of the stack. Measure the sizes of the rivet head and shaft, then drill counterbores (to fit the heads) and shaft holes at each rivet location.
Note: You can purchase special drill bits to make a counterbore and shaft hole in one step.

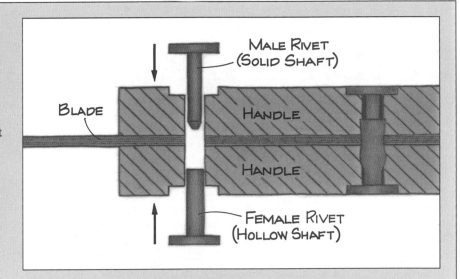

4 **Take the handle blocks apart** and discard the tape. Wrap the sharp edge of the knife blank with masking tape to prevent it from cutting you as you work. Place the handle blocks on either side of the knife blank and line up the rivet holes. Insert the "male" half of a rivet in one end of a rivet hole, and the "female" portion in the other.

5 **Place the assembled handle** on an anvil with one rivet head facing down. Hit the other head with a hammer, driving the two rivet halves together. If necessary, hit the rivet again until the wood and the metal are squeezed together — but don't hammer so hard that the wood splits. Repeat, installing a rivet in each rivet hole.

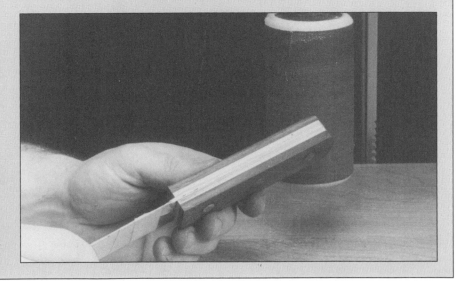

6 **Sand the wooden handle to** its final size and shape, using a disc sander, belt sander, or drum sander. Grind away the wood until it's flush with the metal, but remove as little metal as possible. If you have a "soft-sided" drum sander, use it to round the edges of the handle. When the handle feels comfortable in your hand, sand it smooth and apply a nontoxic finish. Let the finish dry, then remove the masking tape and sharpen the cutting edge of the knife.

11

Butler's Table

In the seventeenth and eighteenth century, well-to-do folks on both sides of the Atlantic Ocean began serving afternoon tea. To facilitate this ritual, craftsmen developed the *butler's table* — a low stand with a detachable top. The top served as a tray; its edges and ends often folded up to prevent the teapot and teacups from sliding off as it was carried about.

The butler's table shown is a contemporary interpretation of the traditional design. The top rests at coffee table height, so the piece can be used in a modern living room or den. There is a shelf below to hold magazines or collectibles. And although the top is detachable, it can be fastened in place with four bolts through the end aprons and cleats.

The table shown was made from oak, which was stained by "fuming" the wood with ammonia. Oak has a high concentration of tannic acid, and when this comes in contact with ammonia vapor (from evaporating household or aqueous ammonia), it turns the wood dark brown. After the oak was fumed, it was coated with spar varnish and rubbed out to a satin gloss.

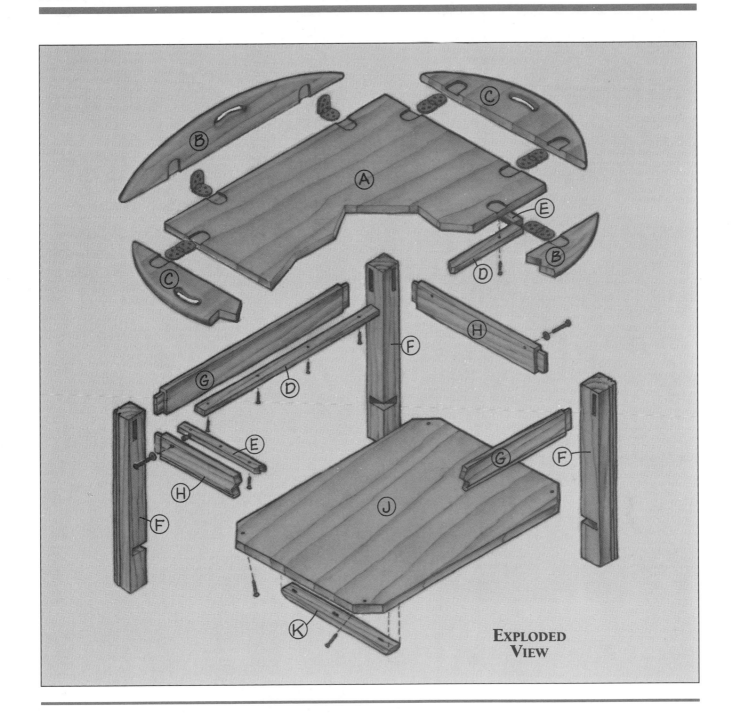

EXPLODED VIEW

MATERIALS LIST (FINISHED DIMENSIONS)

Parts

A.	Top	3/4″ x 16″ x 28″
B.	Side leaves (2)	3/4″ x 4″ x 28″
C.	End leaves (2)	3/4″ x 4″ x 16″
D.	Side cleats (2)	3/4″ x 1″ x 22½″
E.	End cleats (2)	3/4″ x 1″ x 10½″
F.	Legs (4)	2″ x 2″ x 19¼″

G.	Side aprons (2)	3/4″ x 3″ x 24½″
H.	End aprons (2)	3/4″ x 3″ x 12½″
J.	Shelf	3/4″ x 14″ x 26″
K.	Braces (2)	3/4″ x 1¼″ x 10″

Hardware

Butler's tray hinges and mounting screws (8)

#10 x 1¼″ Flathead wood screws (16)

¼″ x 20 Threaded inserts (4)

¼″ x 1¼″ Roundhead stove bolts and washers (4)

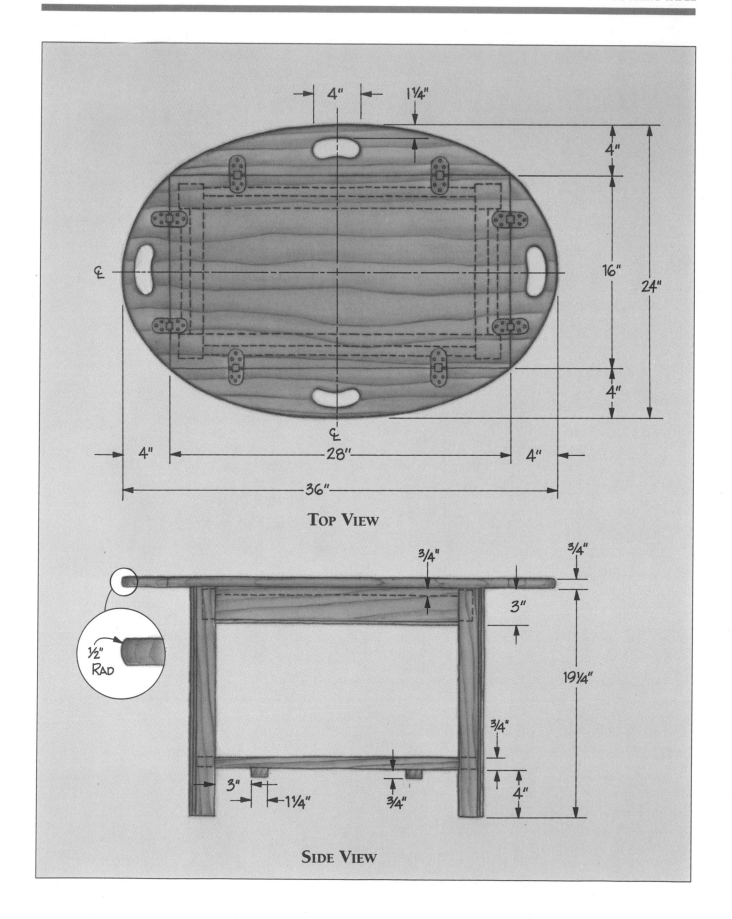

TOP VIEW

SIDE VIEW

PLAN OF PROCEDURE

1 Select the stock and cut the parts to size.
To make this project, you need about 14 board feet of 4/4 (four-quarters) stock and 4 board feet of 10/4 (ten-quarters) stock. Traditionally, butler's tables are made from mahogany, walnut, or cherry. However, you can use almost any cabinet-grade wood. The table shown is made from curly red oak.

Plane the 4/4 stock to ³/₄ inch thick. From this wood, glue up a board 25 inches wide and 37 inches long. Later, you'll cut this in five parts to make the top and the leaves. Also glue up stock to make the shelf. Cut all the ³/₄-inch-thick parts to size *except* the top and leaves.

From the 10/4 stock, cut four pieces about 2¹/₄ inches square and 20 inches long. For each piece, joint two adjacent sides perfectly straight and exactly 90 degrees to one another. Then plane the remaining two sides until the piece is 2 inches thick and wide. When the legs are straight and square, cut them to length.

2 Cut the mortises in the legs. The aprons are joined to the legs with mortises and tenons. Lay out the mortises on each leg, as shown in the *Leg-to-Apron Joinery Detail*. Remove most of the waste from each mortise by drilling a series of overlapping ³/₈-inch-diameter, 1-inch-deep holes, then clean up the ends and edges with a chisel.

3 Cut the tenons in the aprons. Using a dado cutter or a router, cut tenons in the ends of the aprons to fit the leg mortises. Form the cheeks of each tenon by making 1-inch-wide, ³/₁₆-inch-deep rabbets in the apron ends, then cut the steps at the top and bottom of the tenon by making 1-inch-wide, ¹/₄-inch-deep rabbets.

4 Cut the dadoes in the legs. The shelf rests in dadoes in the inside corners of the legs. You must cut these dadoes at a 45-degree angle to the faces. To do this, hold the legs in a V-block as you guide them over a dado cutter or table-mounted router. (*SEE FIGURE 11-1.*)

5 Cut the beads in the legs and aprons. The outside corners of the legs and the bottom edges of the aprons are shaped to form decorative beads. Cut these beads with a molder and beading knives, or you can make a similar shape with a router and a point-cut roundover bit. (*SEE FIGURE 11-2.*)

11-1 Cut the ³/₄-inch-wide, 1¹/₄-inch-deep dadoes that hold the shelf in the legs with a dado cutter or a table-mounted router. Rest each leg in a V-block so the faces are 45 degrees from the surface of the worktable. Position the fence 4 inches away from the cutter or bit, and butt the bottom end of the leg against the fence. Using a miter gauge to guide the V-block, pass the leg over the cutting tool.

11-2 To make the decorative beads in the outside corners of the legs with a molder and beading knives, set up the tool to cut two ³/₁₆-inch beads in one pass. The edge of the outside bead should be flush with the corner of the board. Make a pass, flip the board end for end and turn it 90 degrees, then make another. If you're using a table-mounted router and a point-cut roundover bit, the procedure is similar but you must make several more passes, since you can only cut half a bead with each pass.

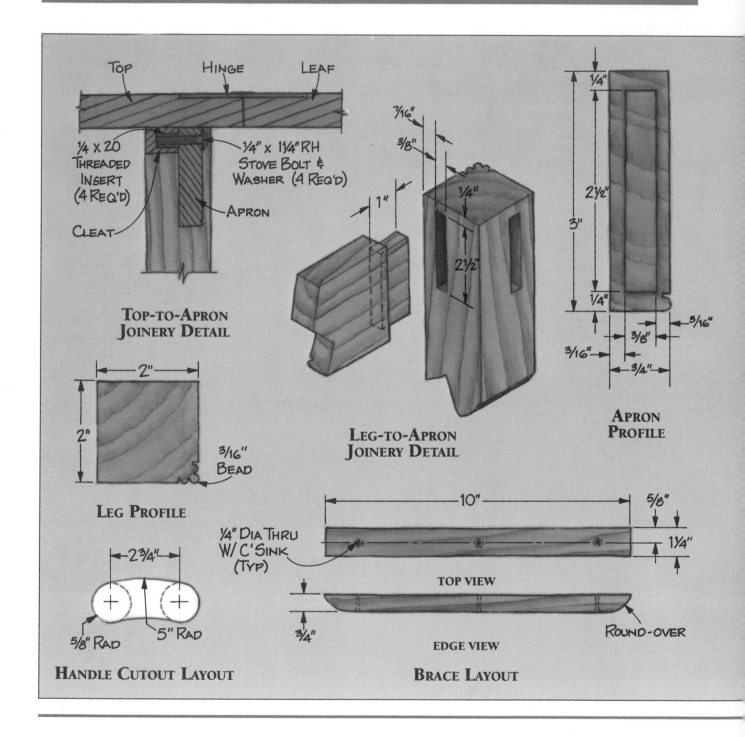

TOP   HINGE   LEAF

1/4 X 20 THREADED INSERT (4 REQ'D)

1/4" x 1 1/4" RH STOVE BOLT & WASHER (4 REQ'D)

APRON

CLEAT

TOP-TO-APRON JOINERY DETAIL

2"

2"

3/16" BEAD

LEG PROFILE

7/16"

3/8"

1"

1/4"

2 1/2"

LEG-TO-APRON JOINERY DETAIL

1/4"

2 1/2"

3"

1/4"

3/16"

3/8"

3/4"

5/16"

APRON PROFILE

2 3/4"

5/8" RAD

5" RAD

HANDLE CUTOUT LAYOUT

1/4" DIA THRU W/ C'SINK (TYP)

10"

5/8"

1 1/4"

TOP VIEW

3/4"

ROUND-OVER

EDGE VIEW

BRACE LAYOUT

6   Drill the holes in the braces and cleats. The braces and end cleats are attached to the underside of the shelf and top with flathead wood screws. The shanks of these screws rest in oversize holes so the wide parts can expand and contract. Drill 1/4-inch-diameter holes with countersinks in the end cleats and braces, as shown in the *Top Layout/Bottom View* and *Brace Layout/Top View*. The positions of these

holes aren't critical, but they should be evenly spaced along the boards.

7   Round the ends of the braces. Round-over the ends of the braces, as shown in the *Brace Layout/ Edge View*. This will make them less noticeable on the assembled project.

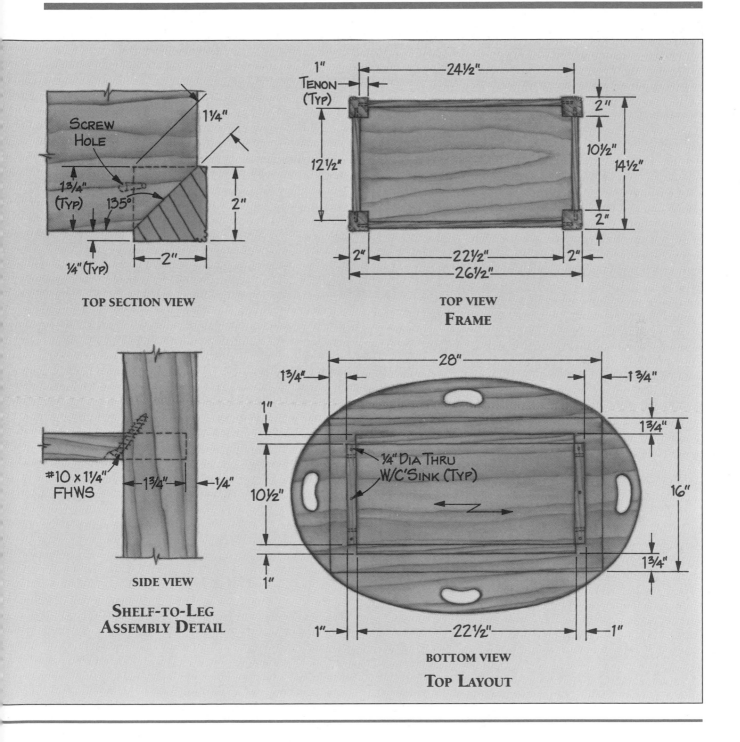

TOP SECTION VIEW

TOP VIEW
FRAME

SIDE VIEW

SHELF-TO-LEG
ASSEMBLY DETAIL

BOTTOM VIEW
TOP LAYOUT

8 Miter the corners of the shelf. Miter the corners of the shelf at 135 degrees, as shown in the *Shelf-to-Leg Assembly Detail/Top Section View*. This fits the shelf to the angled dadoes in the legs.

9 Assemble the base. Finish sand the parts of the table base — legs, aprons, shelf, and braces. Glue the legs to the end aprons, inserting the tenons in the mortises. Let the glue set, then glue together the leg assemblies, side aprons, and shelf. To pin the shelf to the legs, drive flathead wood screws at an angle up through the shelf and into the legs, as shown in the *Shelf-to-Leg Assembly Detail/Side View*. Attach the braces to the underside of the shelf with flathead wood screws, but do *not* glue them in place.

10 **Cut the top and leaves.** Draw a 24-inch-wide, 36-inch-long oval on the stock you glued up to make the top and leaves. *(See Figure 11-3.)* Inside this oval, mark a 20-inch-wide, 28-inch-long rectangle. The corners of this rectangle should touch the oval, as shown in the *Top View* and *Top Layout/Bottom View*.

Rip and crosscut the board into five parts — the top and four leaves. Each of the leaves should be a little more than 4 inches wide. The side leaves must be as long as the top, and the end leaves must be as long as the top is wide.

11 **Make the handles.** Lay out the handle cutouts, as shown in the *Top View* and the *Handle Cutout Layout.* Drill a 1¼-inch-diameter hole at each end of each cutout, then remove the waste between the holes with a saber saw or coping saw. Sand the sawed edges.

12 **Install the hinges in the top and leaves.** Temporarily assemble the top and leaves with bar clamps. Trace the positions of the hinges on the top face, then cut mortises for the hinges with a router and a straight bit. Remove the bar clamps and install the hinges.

13 **Cut the shape of the leaves.** Turn the top assembly over so the underside faces up. Replace the nails in their holes and redraw the oval. Because the saw kerf will have removed some stock, the outline of this second oval should be slightly outside the first. However, the corners of the top should just touch the second oval, as they did the first. Using a band saw or saber saw, cut slightly wide of the second oval. Sand the sawed edges, sanding up to the layout line.

14 **Round-over the edges of the leaves and handles.** Using a router and a ½-inch-radius round-over bit, round the outside edges of the leaves while they are still hinged to the top. Disassemble the leaves from the top, removing the hinges. Round-over the inside edges of the handle cutouts with the same router bit.

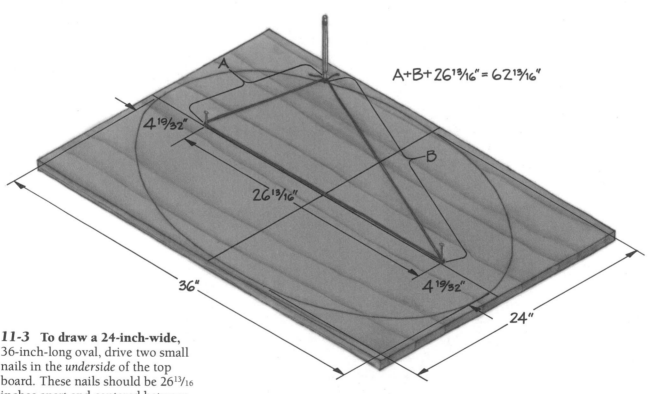

11-3 **To draw a 24-inch-wide,** 36-inch-long oval, drive two small nails in the *underside* of the top board. These nails should be 26¹³/₁₆ inches apart and centered between the edges, as shown. Cut a length of string and tie the ends together to make a loop that's *exactly* 62¹³/₁₆ inches in circumference. Insert the point of a pencil through the knot, then stretch the string over the nails. Draw the oval, keeping the string taut as you pull it around the nails.

15 **Attach the cleats to the top.** Turn the top upside down and center the base on it. Trace the inside edges of the legs and aprons and remove the base. Glue the side cleats to the top, then screw — but do *not* glue — the end cleats in place. Line up the cleats with the lines you've traced so the outside edges of the cleats will be flush with the inside edges of the aprons.

Note: You can glue the side cleats in place because the grain runs parallel to that of the top. But the grain of the end cleats is perpendicular to the top. For this reason, you must attach them with screws, driving the screws through oversize holes. This arrangement keeps the end cleats from restricting the movement of the top. If you were to glue the end cleats in place, the top would soon warp or split.

16 **Fasten the top to the base.** Turn the base and the top right-side up. Place the top on the base with the cleats inside the aprons. Near the ends of each end apron, drill ¼-inch-diameter holes through the aprons and into the end cleats. Remove the top from the base, enlarge the holes in the cleats to ³/₈ inch in diameter, and install threaded inserts in these holes. Replace the top on the base and fasten it by driving roundhead stove bolts through the apron holes and into the threaded inserts in the cleats.

17 **Finish the butler's table.** Although you can apply any type of finish that suits your fancy, the table shown was stained with ammonia and protected with spar varnish. Ammonia fuming will only work with woods that have a high concentration of tannic acid, such as oak and mahogany. If you have used a different wood, you may want to use a different stain — or no stain at all. If you have used an acid-rich wood and want to duplicate the finish shown, follow this finishing schedule:

■ Remove the top from the base. Finish sand the top and leaves, and do any necessary touch-up sanding on the base. All wooden surfaces should be sanded to 180-grit. Vacuum the wood and wipe it with a tack cloth.

■ Using sheets of plastic and long, thin scraps of wood, build a small tent or enclosure *outdoors*. (You can also use the "Portable Finishing Booth" shown on page 79.) Place the base assembly, top assembly, and leaves in this enclosure with a quart of aqueous ammonia in a tempered glass dish. Place the dish on an electric hot plate and adjust the temperature to its lowest setting. As the ammonia evaporates, the fumes will react with the tannic acid in the wood, turning it dark brown.

■ Let the wood bathe in the ammonia fumes for several hours, until it's as dark as you want it. (You may have to replenish the ammonia in the dish from time to time.) If you fume the wood long enough, it will turn almost completely black.

■ Open one side of the enclosure, turn off the hot plate, and let the fumes dissipate in the fresh air.

■ Bring the parts of the table back inside and give the wood a light sanding with 220-grit sandpaper. This will smooth any grain that the ammonia vapors may have raised up. Be careful not to sand through the stained layer of wood. Vacuum the surface and wipe it with a tack cloth.

■ Apply a dark brown wood filler. Let it dry, then sand the surface lightly with 250-grit sandpaper. Vacuum and wipe with a tack cloth.

■ Thin one-half cup of spar varnish with one-half cup of mineral spirits to make a penetrating coat. Wipe it on the wood, then wipe off any excess. Let the varnish dry, then sand it lightly with 320-grit wet/dry sandpaper. Lubricate the paper with mineral spirits.

■ Apply three coats of undiluted spar varnish, brushing the finish on as thin as possible. Let the first and second coats dry overnight, then sand with 400-grit wet/dry sandpaper. After each sanding, vacuum and wipe with a tack cloth.

■ Let the third coat cure for at least a week. Sand with 600-grit wet/dry sandpaper, then rub the coat out with pumice and linseed oil.

■ Apply a coat of paste wax and buff well.

INDEX

Note: Page references in *italic* indicate photographs or illustrations.
Boldface references indicate charts or tables.

WOODWORKING GLOSSARY

TENON DETAIL

CHEEK
SHOULDER

MORTISE
TENON

NOTCH
LAP JOINT

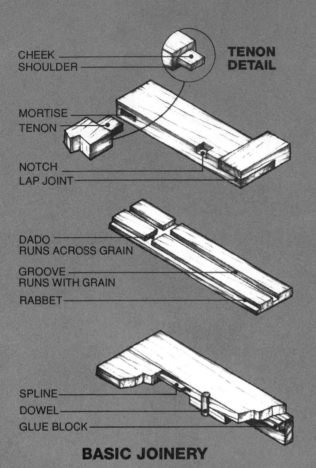

DADO
RUNS ACROSS GRAIN

GROOVE
RUNS WITH GRAIN

RABBET

SPLINE
DOWEL
GLUE BLOCK

BASIC JOINERY

FINGERS

FINGER JOINT

PIN

TAIL

DOVETAIL JOINT

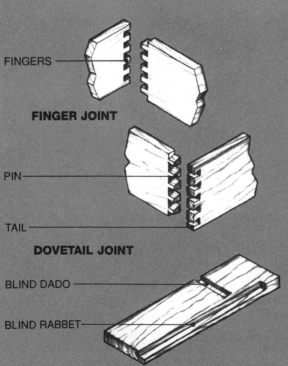

BLIND DADO

BLIND RABBET

SPECIAL JOINERY

STRAIGHT

TAPERED

CABRIOLE

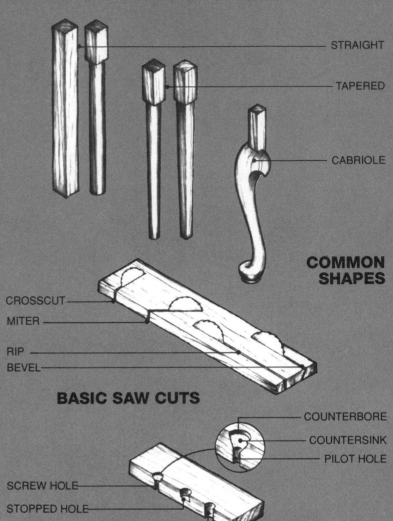

COMMON SHAPES

CROSSCUT
MITER

RIP
BEVEL

BASIC SAW CUTS

COUNTERBORE
COUNTERSINK
PILOT HOLE

SCREW HOLE

STOPPED HOLE

THRU HOLE

HOLES

RADIUS — 1½" RAD   1½" DIA • — ¾" — • DIAMETER

¼" WD X ⅜" DP RABBET

DIMENSION LINE

¼" THK BACK — THICK

36"

32"

GRAIN DIRECTION

HIDDEN LINES

WIDE
¼" WD X ⅜" DP X 8" LG BLIND RABBET — DEEP — LONG

8½"

TYPICAL INDICATES THAT SIMILAR UNMARKED FEATURES ARE THE SAME — ½" (TYP)

3½" (TYP)

CENTERLINE

SECTION LINE INDICATES PLANE OF CROSS SECTION

8½"

¾"

10"

FRONT VIEW   **SIDE VIEW**

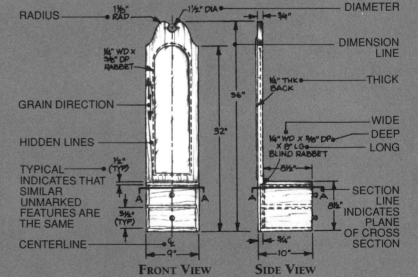

FLATHEAD WOOD SCREW — #3 X ½" FHWS (TYP)

SECTION A
1/16" GAP BETWEEN DRAWER & GLIDE

DENOTES CROSS SECTION

ROUNDHEAD WOOD SCREW — #3 X ½" RHWS

SECTION A

PROJECT PLAN SYMBOLS